WITH SWEET MAJESTY, WARREN E. BURGER

BY
RONALD L. TROWBRIDGE

Published by the
Trust for the Bicentennial of the United States Constitution
November, 2000
Washington, D.C.

To my wife Pamela, who persuaded me that
my memories of the Chief were meant to be shared

ACKNOWLEDGMENTS

My appreciation for those who write many books has increased immeasurably in the writing of this book. While a labor of love, it is a hard business, especially owing to the endless checking of details to ensure accuracy. So a writer needs a lot of help. Quite simply, this book would not have been published without the help of Eva Martin Clark, Jon Corombos, Kemp Harshman, Margie King, Angela Lashaway, Kim Tedders, and Stephanie Umphress. I single out my wife Pamela, because she performed every editorial task there is.

Cover photo provided by the Commission on the Bicentennial of the United States Constitution.

Contents

. . . Oh, now who will behold

The royal captain of this ruined band

Walking from watch to watch, from tent to tent,

Let him cry "Praise and glory on his head!"

For forth he goes and visits all his host,

Bids them good morrow with a modest smile,

And calls them brothers, friends, and countrymen.

Upon his royal face there is no note

How dread an army hath enrounded him.

Nor doth he dedicate one jot of color

Unto the weary and all-watchéd night,

But freshly looks and overbears attaint

With cheerful semblance and sweet majesty,

That every wretch, pining and pale before,

Beholding him, plucks comfort from his looks.

Henry V, IV, Prologue, 28-42

INTRODUCTION

This is a large biographic slice of life. It is not an examination of the Burger Court; I must leave that to legal experts. Rather, it is simply a book about Warren Burger, the man, as I and some of his closest friends came to know him. It is a recording of warm, good-humored, touching, sometimes critical or otherwise human stories, anecdotes, and pleasant recollections about the "Chief," as he liked to be called, who was an intensely private man.

If those of us who knew the Chief well do not record our observations of him as a man, such history will be lost forever—and that would be a pity because he was a gentleman, and a rare statesman whose example as a major leader in the twentieth century needs to be preserved. He was the fifteenth Chief Justice of the United States (there have been 42 presidents), serving for 17 years (1969-1986), longer than any other Chief Justice in the twentieth century. Appointed by the 37th president, Richard Nixon, the Chief left office under the 40th president, Ronald Reagan. He was a statesman, yet he could move easily among ordinary people, and when we ordinary people were with him, we aspired to rise to his level. So he was both above us and among us. Shakespeare captured this paradox precisely: In Act IV of *Henry V*, he describes the captain moving among his troops "with cheerful semblance and sweet majesty."

I worked for or with the Chief from March 1986 until his death June 25, 1995—nine years and four months. In March of 1986, I was interviewed and hired by him for the staff position of Director of Federal and International Programs with the Commission on the Bicentennial of the United States Constitution, which he chaired. After serving in this position for two years, I was appointed Staff Director. I resigned from the Commission on January 6, 1990, but the Chief subsequently appointed me and a few hand-picked friends to the private Trust for the Bicentennial of the United States Constitution that he created for the purpose of continuing the work of the Bicentennial Commission. As his Staff Director for the Commission, I spent nearly two years with the Chief, working with him daily, even on weekends, at his home and in my office, which he visited daily, staying anywhere from one hour to three hours. I traveled with him abroad on two occasions, staying literally in the same room with him, sleeping on the couch. Other than for Burnett Anderson, who was his closest friend since their Harold Stassen days together in Minneapolis, and Judge Michael Luttig, who clerked for him, I knew the Chief perhaps as well and as intimately as anyone. I loved the man, I miss him very much, and I think about him all the time. In my Rolodex is a card with the Chief's home phone and address; I cannot bring myself to throw it away because that would end a chapter that I do not want to end. My book keeps alive his presence. As a man dying of ALS once said to a close friend, "Death ends a life, not a relationship."

For this book I interviewed in 1998 in their offices the following for special reasons:

- Burnett Anderson, because he was the Chief's closest friend and confidant for 54 years. No one was in close second place. Burnett died in 1998 shortly after our interview.

- Judge Michael Luttig, because he was the Chief's closest clerk. Judge Luttig delivered the Chief's principal eulogy at the funeral on June 29, 1995, and he chaired the subsequent "In Memoriam" tribute to the Chief at the Proceedings of the Bar and Officers of the Supreme Court of the United States on April 30, 1996. He was also executor of the Chief's estate.

- Judge Kenneth Starr, because he clerked for two terms for the Chief and developed what he called a "father-to-son" intimacy.

- Lloyd Cutler, because the Chief had selected him to be a member of our moot court team in England and Ireland. From a myriad number of attorneys and judges, the Chief chose Cutler, who had been White House Counsel to President Carter and who would later become White House Counsel to President Clinton.
- Justice Sandra Day O'Connor, because she was one of the Chief's favorite Supreme Court colleagues.

Just before my interview with the Chief in March 1986 for a position on the Bicentennial Commission staff, Mark Cannon, who was then Staff Director and who had been a personal aide to the Chief at the Court for 13 years, gave me some good advice: he told me that the Chief was not impressed with people who are stuck on themselves, who try to impress him with how smart they are. The interview in the Chief's chambers lasted one hour. I spoke for ten minutes; the Chief, fifty. I got the job. The Chief and the bipartisan Bicentennial Commission subsequently selected me Staff Director in 1988.

CHAPTER I

OPINIONS ON CONTROVERSIAL MATTERS

On May 7, 1987, as the Constitution was approaching its bicentennial on September 17, 1987, Supreme Court Justice Thurgood Marshall delivered a speech to a gathering of lawyers in Hawaii. His speech was critical of the Bicentennial Commission's plans and, more pointedly, was critical of the Founding Fathers themselves. Marshall said in remarks printed by the *Washington Post* that he did not "find the wisdom, foresight and sense of justice exhibited by the framers particularly profound." When the Chief was asked to comment on Justice Marshall's criticism, he declined. The next day I took the clipping from the *Post* to my daily meeting with the Chief in my office. I remember my exact words: "Thurgood Marshall's comments about the framers may not be the most inaccurate comment ever made by a member of the Supreme Court, but I do not ever recall *hearing* a comment more inaccurate." I went on to say that to disagree with the framers on the matter of slavery was one issue, but there were reasons why the framers could not outlaw slavery: to do so would have been to defy the South and that would have meant there would have been no Constitution at all. The framers, therefore, had to compromise, with the understanding that the amendment process, which the framers also built into the Constitution, could later solve, resolve, or amend flaws within it. But to suggest that the framers were not particularly profound is grossly off the mark; it was something of a miracle that the framers could design in the period of three short months a Constitution that would govern an entire country and last these two-hundred-plus years. By contrast, attend a session of Congress sometime and see how interminably long it can take to resolve a single issue. While I was opining about Thurgood Marshall, the Chief said nothing—he couldn't, but I could tell by his demeanor that he obviously had a much higher assessment of the value of the framers than did Justice Marshall. The Chief had written in the Preface of the Bicentennial Commission's edition of the Constitution, "This Constitution was not perfect; it is not perfect today even with amendments, but it has continued longer than any other written form of government."

The Chief and I rarely discussed cases pending before the Supreme Court. Whenever I asked his opinion about a certain case, his response was always the same: "I haven't studied the case," which is exactly what a judge ought to say. But I got to know the Chief well enough that he did convey to me his opinions on certain issues. He told me that he believed in some degree of gun control, citing his favorite analogy that just as one could require a license to operate a potentially dangerous automobile, so one also ought to be able to require a license to use a potentially dangerous weapon. He objected to abortion for minors who sought to have it without parental consent. He offered the analogy of a teenager not being able to get her tonsils out without parental consent, yet being able to have a fetus removed without that same consent. This made logically no medical sense to him. He sided with the majority in *Roe v. Wade*, but told me that he thought *Roe v. Wade* ought to be reheard by the Supreme Court. Though he joined with the majority, he was always quick to point out subsequent written dissents. He stated that he did not intend *Roe v. Wade* to be unmitigated abortion on demand. On the matter of flag burning, he defined such action as "conduct" rather than "speech" or "expression" and cited Hugo Black's position, who was an ardent defender of the First Amendment and yet who opposed the burning of the flag and found such actionable.

At the Chief's memorial tribute, Solicitor General Drew Days noted:

> In 1973, he joined in the Court's landmark Due Process opinion in *Roe v. Wade*, a decision that was to become one of the most controversial in the Court's history. In a separate concurrence, however, he warned against reading "sweeping consequences" into the holding, emphasizing that it did not advance the idea that the Constitution required abortion on demand. In a dissent some years later, he was to express misgiving about the *Roe* decision, fearing that it had paved the way for the Court to go beyond the limits commanded by the Constitution:
>
> > "[E]very Member of the *Roe* Court rejected the idea of abortion on demand. The Court's opinion today, however, plainly undermines that important principle, and I regretfully conclude that some of the concerns of the dissenting Justices in *Roe*, as well as the concerns I expressed in my separate concurrence, have now been realized."

Judge Robert Bork clarified a major misunderstanding at this same memorial tribute:

> It is always a little more difficult to assess a Chief Justice's work because, when a majority he disagrees with has the votes, with or without his vote, he may join that majority in order to assign the opinion and limit the damage to the law. Some of Warren Burger's votes that have been described as liberal activism are due to that tactic.

On the matter of legal ethics, the Chief was outspoken, nearly to the point of apoplexy, about attorneys who advertise in the media. And he was equally apoplectic about prosecutors and defense attorneys who argue their cases in the public media. He wanted to protect the integrity of the judicial process and therefore thought that all Supreme Court trials should be closed to the media. Justice was the end, not politics or the histrionics of courtroom performance.

When I asked the Chief his opinion of Robert Bork, whom President Reagan had nominated for the Supreme Court, he told me and later said on USIA's Worldnet, which was an international broadcast, that "Judge Bork was the best-qualified candidate for the Supreme Court in the past 50 years." He also made that same evaluation before the Senate Judiciary Committee, in the presence of Senator Kennedy, who was leading the charge against Judge Bork's nomination. Senator Kennedy also served on the Bicentennial Commission, but the Chief did a masterfully diplomatic job of maintaining peace and decorum there with such diverse members as liberal Ted Kennedy, conservative Phyllis Schlafly, and libertarian Bernard Siegan, Siegan being a candidate for a federal judgeship whom Ted Kennedy aggressively attacked. The Chief, as chairman, would never permit the Commission's activities and publications to degenerate into political controversy; instead, he stated repeatedly that ours was to be a "history and civics lesson for all." He would not allow any Republican or Democrat or liberal or conservative to run with the Commission in any direction. On one occasion, Senator Kennedy, who was a member of the international committee of the Bicentennial commission, requested a staff-only meeting in a location apart from Commission headquarters. It seemed clandestine, so I reported it to the Chairman of the Commission, as I was charged always to do when contacted on a substantive matter by a Commissioner. The Chief, without invitation, showed up at Senator Kennedy's meeting, with happy demeanor, and defused what may or may not have been an effort to put a political slant on Commission activities. I can also say without hesitation that had Phyllis Schlafly attempted to hold a meeting in a similar vein, the Chief would have showed up to that one as well to preempt any kind of political excursion. Our approach was history, not politics.

Now comes a story that reflects the best of Chief Justice Warren Burger and in some ways the worst of Congress. On July 21, 1989, the Bicentennial Commission received a request from Rep. Fortney "Pete" Stark's office for several boxes of pocket Constitutions. As always, we happily delivered the boxes, wishing to get as many copies of the Constitution out to the public as possible. We didn't care who took the credit. We were surprised to receive the following letter from Mr. Stark:

> Dear Mr. Chief Justice:
> Thank you for the kind delivery of several boxes of materials. It is a generous offer. However, in the name of eliminating duplicative or unnecessary government spending, I must respectfully decline the acceptance of the offer. I would appreciate, if possible, if you could have your staff confirm with my office if there is a need for additional materials before the delivery of such materials takes place in the future.

The Chief was not about to acquiesce to false charges. I initially drafted the Chief's response as follows:

> Dear Mr. Stark:
> I have your letter of August 8 (copy attached) in which you decline "in the name of eliminating duplicative or unnecessary government spending" to accept several boxes of materials we sent your office. We sent these materials upon a telephone request on July 21 from a staff member in your office.
> Either I or someone on our staff will call to ensure that the matter is satisfactorily resolved.

The Chief made my draft much stronger (Figure 1):

> Dear Mr. Stark:
> I have your curiously worded letter of August 8 (copy attached) in which you decline "in the name of eliminating duplicative or unnecessary government spending" to accept several boxes of materials we sent

Supreme Court of the United States
Washington, D. C. 20543

CHAMBERS OF
CHIEF JUSTICE BURGER
RETIRED

August 29, 1989

Dear Mr. Stark: *curiously worded*

I have your ∧letter of August 8 (copy attached) in which you decline "in the name of eliminating duplicative or unnecessary government spending" to accept several boxes of material we sent you ~~you~~ *an* ~~office.~~ We sent these materials upon a telephone request on July 21 ~~from a staff member in your~~ ~~office.~~ *from my own office.*

Either I or someone on our staff will ~~call~~ to *be available* ~~insure that the matter is satisfactorily resolved.~~ *assure that the "right hand" in your staff will know what the ~~left~~ some of the other hands are doing..*

Chairman
Commission on the Bicentennial
of the U.S. Constitution

Honorable Pete Stark
House of Representatives
Washington, D.C. 20515.

P I do not regard it as a "waste" of government money to make 10 & copies of the Const. available to ... many Americans .. possible.. Respectfully

Figure 1

you on a telephone request from your office on July 21.

Either I or someone on our staff will be available to assure that the "right hand" on your staff will know what some of the other hands are doing.

I do not regard it as a "waste" of government money to make 10-cent copies of the Constitution available to as many Americans as possible.

It must be remembered that Mr. Stark had sometimes leaked letters to the media for personal advantage. When Malcolm Forbes, for example, threw his two-million-dollar birthday party in Morocco, Mr. Stark wrote the IRS demanding that Forbes not be allowed any business deductions for his party. His letter was leaked to the press; it played well back in his district.

I asked the Chief if I could send his exchange with Mr. Stark to the *Washington Post*. He mumbled indifference.

The *Post* featured the exchange prominently:

Returned Copies of Constitution Inspire Broadside From Burger

When it comes to the Constitution and former chief justice Warren E. Burger, there's no fooling around.

That's apparently what prompted Burger to fire off an angry letter last week to Rep. Fortney "Pete" Stark (D-Calif.). Sources at the Commission on the Bicentennial of the Constitution, which Burger heads, said "the chief" was incensed that Stark had returned 1,000 copies of the Constitution to the agency, "in the name of eliminating duplicative or unnecessary spending."

In a three-paragraph letter on Supreme Court letterhead, Burger told Stark that someone on his staff had requested the materials earlier this summer. "Either I or someone on our staff will be available to assure that the 'right hand' on your staff will know what some of the other hands are doing," Burger said.

"I do not regard it as a 'waste' of government money to make 10-cent copies of the Constitution available to as many Americans as possible," he told Stark.

A spokesman for Stark said he had no comment on why the congressman had rejected the copies.

The furies broke loose. I received a phone call from a Stark aide demanding in no uncertain terms to see our records. "We did not order the Constitutions," he said. Yes they did; we kept records of date and time. The Stark aide then, without invitation, burst into Commission headquarters demanding to see me, literally pounding the walls so hard as to cause pictures to fall off. What this aide did not know was that at that moment Chief Justice Burger was sitting in my office. "Ron, what's that noise?" "Chief, it's Pete Stark's staff." I will never forget what followed: the Chief sat up erect and said, "Why don't you have him arrested?"

Because of the *Post's* disclosure, a few Congressman called with requests, such as, "Those Constitutions that Pete Stark didn't want, I'll take 'em." Then, a short time later, a columnist for Jack Anderson marched unannounced into Commission headquarters, declaring that he had it from a reliable member of Congress that the Commission had abused its travel budget and he wanted to see all our records. What Stark didn't know in this fishing expedition was that Chief Justice Burger was incredibly frugal and personally cleared all requests for staff travel, which he rarely allowed. With, or even without, the Freedom of Information Act, we were pleased to open our public books; Anderson's reporter found nothing.

Poetic justice would triumph in yet another way. Mr. Stark had been battling the National Rifle Association on the Second Amendment, when, coincidentally, the exposé appeared in the *Post* suggesting that Stark regarded the Constitution as a waste. The NRA reprinted the *Post* piece in its *American Rifleman* magazine that went to some three million subscribers. Stark's staff called me frantically, saying they were being besieged by thousands of protesting calls and letters from NRA members and, believe it or not, would I "issue a retraction"? I reminded them that I did not write Stark's letter to the Chief.

Finally, Mr. Stark sent the following letter (September 13, 1989) to

Senator Ernest Hollings, Chairman of the Subcommittee on Commerce, Justice, State and Judiciary, requesting that the bipartisan Bicentennial Commission be terminated promptly:

> Dear Mr. Chairman:
>
> I hope you can reduce or even eliminate the appropriation for the Commission on the Bicentennial of the U.S. Constitution. It would be a great place to make savings to pay for the anti-drug war or meet Gramm-Rudman targets. The House has approved some $14 million in FY 1990 for them. FY 1990, by the way, will be the 203 anniversary of the Constitutional Convention—how long does this have to go on?
>
> I had a run-in with Chairman Burger and am upset about their treatment of the public, about their attitude toward trying to save money, and about the waste that one of my staff saw there. Send one of your Appropriations staffers down unannounced and see what it looks like. They don't need $14 million or nearly a $1000 a day in travel!
>
> It is a great place to save some money for the anti-drug effort or other matters being requested of the Appropriations Committee.
>
> Thank you for your consideration.

When Senator Kennedy received of a copy of this letter, one of his staff, in jocular disbelief, forwarded a copy to the Chief. Stark was requesting that Kennedy put himself as commissioner, the bipartisan Commission, and the commemoration of our Constitution out of business. What was refreshing was Chief Justice Burger's honest, principled courage to rebuke rightfully in writing a powerful majority member of Congress. My nine years in Washington working at a high Executive-Branch level told me that not many Reagan or Bush administrators would have had the courage to confront a majority Congressman as Warren Burger had. Would that there were more of these rare statesmen. It is too often Stark's rather than the Chief's example that triumphs.

CHAPTER 2

"INVASION OF THE BRITISH ISLES"

The Chief and I journeyed to England on two different occasions, each time staying at the Marriott, in Grosvenor Square near the American Embassy. Both times, the Chief had called his friend Bill Marriott and persuaded him to give us the suite at the cost of tax only. So this suite, which ran about $500 a night, cost us instead about $71 tax per night. Memorable incidents occurred at the Marriott. He slept in the bedroom, I on the sofa, and I agreed to wake him the next morning at nine. Breakfast arrived and we sat eating and drinking coffee until—noon. He recreated during that time story after story of his experiences with people like President Nixon, Gorbachev, and Khruschev; it was a fascinating personal history lesson for me. As we sat there for hours, he, in time, removed from the breakfast basket the rolls and jars of jellies that remained, carefully putting them on a shelf to be eaten later. He knew that if they were returned to the kitchen, they would be discarded. He was, we must remember, a child of the Depression and had learned to be frugal and not waste things. That night, he washed by hand his white, drip-dry shirt and hung it in the shower to dry.

My first trip abroad with the Chief was on November 21-27, 1987, on the occasion of his delivering the Churchill Lecture. Had he still been Chief Justice, he would, on arrival in London, have been accorded VIP, official government treatment—an official escort quickly off the plane and out of the airport, bypassing customs and the gathering of luggage. However, he had resigned the year before, and now he would have to get off the plane and be treated as an ordinary traveler. I knew this would be the case from my years at the United States Information Agency, working with embassies abroad. So, believing that he should still be accorded some VIP treatment, I contacted the American Embassy in advance of our trip and asked kindly if they would provide VIP service for the Chief. They were happy to do so. When we boarded the plane at Dulles, I was very happy I had made that call because coincidentally Charles H. Price II, Ambassador to England, was traveling to London also. He definitely would receive VIP treatment, and the lack of it for the Chief would have been very sad. When we arrived at London Heathrow airport, we were met by Darrell Mills from the Embassy with an Embassy car. We did not get quite the treatment accorded Ambassador Price, but we did get treatment that was commensurate with the historical integrity of the former Chief Justice of the United States.

For both ends of the 1987 trip, I arranged with officials at Dulles airport to get him through the airport without going through the magnetometers, which he always refused to pass through as a matter of principle. On the flight back from London, the Chief rode first class and I, coach class. Because of his polio, the three-inch curvature of his spine and the chronic pain, he needed to ride first class so that he could stretch his legs out unimpeded. Even with the comfort of first class he was still in chronic pain, but he always managed to endure, complaining very little about it. In coach class, but not far from him, I heard him politely ask the flight attendant if his aide might join him since the seat next to him was unoccupied. The flight attendant assented. On this return trip, the film *The Untouchables* was showing, starring Kevin Costner as Elliot Ness. Near the end of the film is a lengthy trial scene. The Chief watched it and exclaimed in disbelief that the trial had no relationship to reality. He kept talking to the screen, "You can't do that in a court." Or, "That kind of thing is not permissible." When the plane landed at Dulles, I quickly shot out of my seat, to which the Chief responded that we should sit down and relax because a U.S.

Marshall would arrive soon to escort us out. (Supreme Court Justices are given protection by the U.S. Marshall Service, just as United States presidents and vice presidents receive Secret Service protection.) The Chief continued to receive, despite being out of office, protection, given that a number of death threats had been issued against him when he was Chief Justice. It was also an amenity he had earned after 34 years of public government service.

In May of 1988, we returned to England to conduct moot court cases. Our party consisted of Herbert Brownell, Attorney General under President Eisenhower; Lloyd Cutler, former Counsel to President Carter; Robert Clare, former President of the American College of Trial Lawyers; Richard Morris, Professor of History at Columbia University; and Thomas O'Connor, Professor of History at Boston College. We conducted the moot court cases at the University of Oxford, again at the Middle Temple in London, and at the University of Dublin in Ireland. The moot court case was drawn from *Goldwater v. Carter* and focused on the power of the President to cancel treaties without consent of Congress, and conversely, on the right of Congress to demand confidential documents from the Executive. The three American judges—O'Connor, Morris, and Burger—joined three distinguished British judges: Lord Bridge, Lord Wilberforce and Sir Browne-Wilkinson.

Preceding the moot court case, Chief Justice Burger spoke on the historical setting prior to the Constitutional Convention in 1787; Richard Morris then covered the Convention, followed by Thomas O'Connor who spoke on the Ratification. In the moot court case, Herbert Brownell represented the Executive, Robert Clare, the Secretary of State, and Lloyd Cutler, the Senate. I acted as the Clerk of the Court. I was to give all participants exactly equal time in their presentations, holding up a variety of warning signs and a final sign to let them know that time was up. Herb Brownell ran over the time, so

I determined that Lloyd Cutler would be allowed to run equally over time. Later on the Chief asked me if I had given Lloyd Cutler too much time. I told him that I had, but that it was the same amount of time precisely that Herb Brownell had taken. The Chief did not further dispute the matter. Following the moot court case, the session was open for questions from the audience, composed of jurists, historians, political scientists, lawyers and the academic community. The entire proceedings were videotaped.

CHAPTER 3

BATTLES WITH THE PRESS

An article by Martin Tolchin appeared in *The New York Times* that was, in part, critical of the Chief. Normally, the Chief did not respond to criticisms, but in this case, since it was the reputation of the Commission that was being attacked, he felt obliged to set the record straight. So he wrote a detailed response, asking that it go over my signature rather than his. This is the first time that the Chief Justice was a ghost writer for me! I cite the entire letter because it is a tidy summary of the highlights of the Commission's achievements up to September 1989 and of what the Chief valued. The Chief wrote every word of it:

> Dear Mr. Tolchin:
>
> It has come to our attention in the volume of *Representative American Speeches*, page 11, that you reported in *The New York Times* views of "a number of leading historians" who complain that the Commission of the Bicentennial of the Constitution's efforts focus on "bread and circuses" at the expense of serious scholarship and works of lasting value.
>
> It should be clear by now, but in any event we undertake to emphasize, that their criticism was very wide of the mark and perhaps was directed at what observers noted about events in Philadelphia on September 17, 1787. Of course, if they are truly historians as the article suggested, they should know that there was great celebration, parades and fireworks in Philadelphia on that day in 1787. However, whatever occurred there in 1787 is also beside the point because these events were under the control of the Philadelphia City Commission and beyond the jurisdiction of the national commission.
>
> From the outset, Chief Justice Burger as Chairman of the Commis-

sion had laid down a policy, unanimously adopted by the Commission, that this should be a history and civics lesson for all of us, and, particularly, for young people. A tiny part of the appropriated funds for the Bicentennial Commission has been used for fireworks and parades, but over the last three years, the great preponderance of our financial resources and staff efforts have gone into educational programs, covering the entire spectrum from elementary to adult and continuing education. Enclosed is a leaflet describing some of our current projects in these areas.

Early on, the Commission decided to place the major emphasis of its educational programming on elementary and secondary education. We saw this as the area of the greatest present need and the greatest long-term investment. Moreover, other Federal entities such as Project '87 were already doing much in the area of scholarly research and teaching at the college level, which is not to say that the Commission had not done much by itself in this area. We have given grants to teachers' groups to conduct seminars to "teach the teachers" to help make up for the neglect in history in grade schools and high schools—and even in colleges. We have recognized and encouraged a number of scholarly endeavors through Project Recognition, Project Registry, Bicentennial Campus, and other programs. We have assisted in the distribution of outstanding books to libraries and schools nationwide (e.g., the late Professor Richard Morris's *Framing of the Federal Constitution*). Our Education staff, which includes a professional historian and political scientist, routinely serve as advisors to scholarly projects undertaken outside the Commission.

We have distributed Jeffrey St. John's *Constitutional Journal* to 35,000 high school, college, law, and court libraries. Harcourt Brace has recently published a series of constitutional vignettes written by Chief Justice Burger, available as a textbook to schools and libraries nationwide. The Commission has committed a substantial portion of its financial resources to a College-Community Forums program, which brings academic and lay communities together to examine constitutional issues of importance. A great many scholars have worked on a wide range of Commission projects in both an advisory and participatory capacity. The Commission is funding several major research projects, including an Encyclopedia of Congress, being undertaken by the University of Texas and Lyndon Baines Johnson

Library, the Documentary History of the First Federal Congress at George Washington University, and an upcoming book on the role of the states in the history of our Bill of Rights. Moreover, even our major celebratory activities such as the Celebration of Citizenship and the recent reenactment of George Washington's inaugural have included a significant educational component in publications and the organized involvement of schools.

In addition, in 1987 there was a high school essay contest on the separation of powers which had neither parades nor "circuses" but which reached most of the high schools in the United States. The winners of those contests at the state level received substantial prizes and were given a free trip to Washington. In Washington they met with the leaders of Congress, they were received at the White House by the President and they had a luncheon at the Supreme Court. Fifty-two winners of the essay contest were then designated as delegates to a reenactment of the Constitutional Convention free of adult supervision, which took place over three days in Williamsburg, Virginia. The structure of the meeting was arranged by members of the faculty of the College of William and Mary.

In the current year there was a historical-pictorial map contest in which thousands of students took part in three different sections. An entire class from the fourth grade through the seventh grade would participate, illustrating in whatever way they desired events relating to the Constitution beginning after the Battle of Yorktown in 1781 and the final modification of the Articles of Confederation. Class groups from the seventh, eighth and ninth grades were in separate contests with the same standards. High school students could enter individually. If you are in Washington sometime, drop in at Commission headquarters and you will be astonished at the work of children who will never forget at least the geography of the 13 original colonies and the important dates and events in that period.

The next time you talk with those "leading historians" ask them to find out what's going on so that they can form their judgments on the basis of facts.

Sincerely,

Ron Trowbridge

Staff Director

Another criticism of the Chief appeared in the *Washington Post*. This time I wrote the response, writing first to the Chief on February 1, 1989, "Chief, I would like to submit the attached to the *Post* unless you forbid it. It is perhaps too informal and personal for your taste, but perhaps as such will then get printed. You seem to be the nationwide lightning rod for much criticism and somebody has to set the factual record straight." He considered the piece I was about to send, then added his own revisions, making my initial letter even stronger in tone (Figure 2):

COMMISSION ON THE BICENTENNIAL
OF THE UNITED STATES CONSTITUTION

FEBRUARY 1, 1989
LETTERS TO THE EDITOR
WASHINGTON POST

Dear Editor:

Mark Twain once observed of a critic on one of James Fennimore Cooper's novels that before condemning the book he ought first to have read it. Those accusing Chief Justice Burger of retirement ought first to know, factually, what he does. When he was hospitalized recently for mild pneumonia, dehydration, and "bicentennial exhaustion," he returned early to work anyway, confessing, "My doctors will be angry." He also reported that his doctor threatened no longer to be his doctor if his stubbornness to overwork persists. The Puritan work ethic permeates every bone. We cannot get him to take a vacation, some of us on the staff pushing it so that we can take one.

The Chairman of the Bicentennial Commission works about 60 hours a week, not as a sitting judge, but as a full time plus promoter of the Constitution, a document which created the courts in the first place.

My intention in writing this will, of course, be suspect because of my relationship in substance as "Chief of Staff" to the man, but I recite only what I know daily to be true. To those who continue to suggest that he is

February 1, 1989

Dear Editor:

Mark Twain once observed of a critic on one of James Fennimore Cooper's novels that before condemning the book he ought first to have read it. Those accusing Chief Justice Burger of retirement ought first to know, factually, what he does. When he was hospitalized recently for mild pneumonia, dehydration, and "bicentennial exhaustion," he returned early to work anyway, confessing, "My doctors will be angry with me." He also reported that his doctor threatened no longer to be his doctor if his stubbornness to over work persists. The ~~German~~ Puritan work ethic permeates every bone. We cannot get him to take a vacation, some of us on the staff pushing it so that we ~~plus~~ can take one.

The Chairman of the Bicentennial Commission works about 60 hours a week, not as a sitting judge, but as a full time promoter of the Constitution, a document which ~~enables judges to sit in~~ *created* the first place. ~~His is the horse before the cart. He has~~ ~~donated about $100,000 of his own money to the commemoration~~ of ~~the Constitution, from the salary he does not make at the~~ *in substance as Chief of Staff* ~~Commission.~~

My intention in writing this will, of course, be suspect because of my relationship to the man, but I recite only what I know daily to be true. To those who continue to suggest that he is unemployed, I am reminded of Dr. Johnson's response, "A man might write such stuff forever, if he would abandon his mind to it."

Sincerely,

Ronald L. Trowbridge
Staff Director

RLT:jh

It also reminds of the late Roy Howard's dicta that too much focus on the facts by reporters has ruined many a news story. It is surprising that the Assoc Press can't even get its facts straight.

Figure 2

unemployed, I am reminded of Dr. Johnson's response, "A man might write such stuff forever, if he would abandon his mind to it." It also reminds us of the late Roy Howard's dicta that too much focus on the facts by reporters has ruined many a news story.

It is surprising that the Associated Press can't even get its facts straight.

Sincerely,
Ron Trowbridge

The Commission sponsored the so-called "Magna Carta Freedom Trailer Project," which was a trailer specially equipped to house one of the four remaining Magna Cartas, sent to the Commission on loan from Lincoln Cathedral in England. In the trailer were also other precious displays regarding the Constitution and documents related to Magna Carta and the relationship between the Constitution and Magna Carta. It was an immense project; the trailer was to be sent on a six-month tour to nearly 100 cities in 25 states. The tour was launched at the Rose Garden by President Reagan and Chief Justice Burger. The media were invited. I recall sitting in the Rose Garden with the press cordoned off behind me, within yelling distance of the President. After President Reagan and Chief Justice Burger spoke, the President began walking toward the Oval Office, at which point Sam Donaldson and Bill Plante began shouting questions at him. Not a single one related to the purpose at hand, that is, the celebration of Magna Carta and the Constitution. The next day in the newspapers and on television not a single reference was made to the launching ceremony. The Chief thought it outrageous that the press paid absolutely no attention whatsoever to Magna Carta or its significance to the history of our Constitution.

CHAPTER 4

CHARITY, HUMOR, AND CHILDREN

The Chief gave me a copy of remarks he had delivered at Ripon College, Ripon, Wisconsin, on May 21, 1967, when he was a member of the U.S. Court of Appeals. This was the speech that President Nixon subsequently read in *Ripon Magazine* and used primarily as the main reason he selected Warren Burger to be Chief Justice. I asked the Chief whether Nixon and he had been friends or whether there was some other reason Nixon had appointed him Chief Justice and he said no, that the reason for the selection owed chiefly to this one article.

Some passages in the article might today be regarded as the sentiments of a bleeding-heart liberal. The following is an example:

> The imbalance in our system of criminal justice must be corrected so that we give at least as much attention to the defendant after he is found guilty as before. We must examine into the causes and consequences of the protracted warfare our system of justice fosters. Whether we find it palatable or not, we must proceed, even in the face of bitter contrary experiences, in the belief that every human being has a spark somewhere hidden that will make it possible for redemption and rehabilitation. If we accept the idea that each human, however "bad," is a child of God, we must look for that spark.

He was, of course, here arguing that even the most hardened criminal has a spark of goodness that we must look for. The Chief told me that he personally opposed capital punishment, but believed that the Constitution permitted it, so he would therefore put aside his private feelings in support of the Constitution. After reading this and other passages, I blurted out to the Chief, not entirely in jest, "Chief, you're a closet liberal!" I will never forget his exact response: He said with a devilish, enigmatic grin on his face, "Tell Ted, but don't tell Phyllis"—referring to Ted Kennedy and Phyllis Schlafly, members of the Bicentennial Commission.

The final paragraphs of his Ripon speech contained sentiments commanding our respect:

> Should you come to the conclusion, as you watch our system of justice work, that we lawyers have built up a process that is inadequate or archaic or which is too cumbersome or too complex, or if you think we have carried our basic principle too far, or if for any reason you think the system does not meet the tests of social utility and fairness, you have a remedy. You have the right and the ultimate power to change it. Neither the laws nor the Constitution are too sacred to change—we have changed the original Constitution more than 20 times—and the decisions of judges are not Holy Writ. These things are a means to an end, not an end in themselves. They are tools to serve you, not masters to enslave you.
>
> Some of the elders may wonder whether the next generation, whose activities we see portrayed daily in unflattering settings, will be concerned with these problems. I think you will.
>
> I reject the idea that your generation as a whole is the Alienated Generation; on the contrary, there is much more evidence that you are the Involved Generation—one which has shown a unique quality which has too long been missing in American life. It is a quality which leads young people away from getting rich and advertising agencies and banks and brokers' offices, and into work with human beings through agencies like the Peace Corps and in Government service. In this unique quality lies the hope—indeed the best hope—to relieve the dismal picture I have been discussing.
>
> The missionary zeal of your generation may find solutions. This is your country, these are your times. Get involved.

What I here admire was the Chief's commitment to public service at the expense of personal wealth. I asked him once what he was making yearly in private law practice when he accepted President Eisenhower's appointment in 1953. I cannot recall the exact amount, but I do recall he was making a relative fortune at that time (in the six figures), but he was willing to abandon that for a draconian pay cut in a position with the government. The disparity in the salaries was shocking. But the Chief, as the Ripon speech reflected, was committed to getting involved and serving his country. That is why, near the end of his life when he was no longer Chief Justice and when protocol amenities or perks were no longer given him, I thought such ingratitude disgraceful. That is also why I sometimes went out of my way to buy and pay for certain amenities so that the Chief and the office of Chief Justice would not be demeaned. But I must say, he seemed more willing to be demeaned than I was willing to allow him to be. So I paid for some amenities, such as a limousine to meet him on the tarmac, and simply didn't tell him that I had done so. He showed me a letter once that Lord Hailsham had written him, describing the abrupt termination of amenities once he was out of office. I did not want that same abandonment to happen to Chief Justice Warren Burger. He deserved better.

The same way I could in jest call him a closet liberal, I could kid the Chief in good humor, and he would make light fun of me. He would point his index finger at me with his thumb up, forming a gun, and then pull the trigger. He seemed austere to everyone, but he really had a delightful sense of dry, witty humor. Former Director of the FBI and CIA, William Webster narrates a charming example:

> One warm summer evening in Washington, the Chief and Vera came over for a summer cookout along with then Solicitor General Wade McCree and Doris. I realized that I had no wine in the house for this Chevalier du

Tastevin. Then I remembered that I had one bottle of red wine given me by a farmer who lived near my farm in Missouri. It was a new winery and the wine was only a few months old.

I explained to the Chief that the bottle came from the "other" Williamsburg—Williamsburg, Missouri—near where Winston Churchill delivered his "Iron Curtain" speech, and I asked him to evaluate it. "Well," said the Chief, "let's decant it." I said "fine" although I knew it wasn't old enough to have any sediment. So we let it breathe a bit and then the Chief smelled the cork, held the glass to the light and tasted its contents with obvious skill. I held my breath. Finally he said, with a twinkle in his eyes, "Now this is an unusual wine. It has an interesting impertinence." Those who focused upon his impressive "studio-casting" appearance missed the essence of this very human, fun-loving, caring and loyal man.

Col. Patrick O'Meara, the Bicentennial Commission's head of administrative matters, relates a story of the Chief as a caring man:

In June, 1993, when one of the Chief's law clerks, Carl Tillman, was getting ready to leave, one who had been particularly good to me, I felt obligated to do something for him, so decided to have a cookout in my backyard. We invited the Chief, Carl Tillman's family, and the new clerk coming in and a few people from the Commission. The minute the Chief walked in, he handed me a bottle of champagne in a wicker basket. He indicated to me that it had come from the Shah of Iran, that it was mine and he hoped I'd enjoy it. Of course, it was Dom Perignon, 1985, which I have to this day. He said he and his wife could stay only for 15 minutes, that they had other things they needed to do. It was around 12:30 when they arrived. He looked at our antiques and was very impressed with the stereoscope; both he and Mrs. Burger loved antiques. The two of them went to the backyard, and Mrs. Burger got on the glider while the Chief went to a comfortable chair. They stayed for four hours.

The Chief's thoughtfulness of others also manifested itself in another way. We wanted to celebrate the Chief's 87th birthday on September 17, 1994, to mark not only his birthday, but the 207th anniversary of our Constitution. It is, by the way, a remarkable coincidence that his birthday, September 17, is precisely the birthday of the Constitution; that coincidence must have been preordained. To honor the Chief, Burnett Anderson, Mike Luttig, and I wished to arrange for a reverential roast at the City Tavern Club in Georgetown, one of the Chief's favorite inns because some of the Founding Fathers had dined and stayed there. Burnett, Mike and I each drew up short guest lists and presented them to the Chief. I should have known the idea was doomed at that point: the Chief, who was ever the statesman, diplomat and gentleman, began to think about all the people who were not invited and soon began to worry about all the noses that would be out of joint if they heard about the roast but were excluded from it. He said that if he invited any of his clerks, he must invite them all; that if he invited a judge, he must invite them all, and on and on. It soon became apparent to us that, were we to invite all individuals in town who needed to be invited, we might as well have held the roast in the Redskins' football stadium. We therefore had to abandon the project. I wish now, in retrospect, that we had gone forward with it and perhaps even taken some of the heat from the Chief, because that turned out to be his last birthday. He died nine months later.

The Chief especially cared for children. I heard him say more than once, not entirely in jest, that "once people reach fifty, it's too late." Whenever he read anything that came from a child, almost without fail, tears would come to his eyes. He loved to be in the presence of children and to hear from them. The Department of Education sponsored a Bicentennial essay contest for children, subsequently compiling these essays into a book, and for this book the Chief wrote the following "Message":

MESSAGE
WARREN E. BURGER
Chairman,
Commission on the Bicentennial of the United States Constitution
Chief Justice of the United States, 1969-1986.

I have long believed that discussions of the Constitution should not be limited just to lawyers, since the Constitution is for all of the people. After all, the Constitution's Preamble begins with the words, "WE THE PEOPLE."

During this Bicentennial celebration, we especially hope to stimulate the young. The 150 pieces in this volume demonstrate that children of all ages can understand the underlying purposes of the Constitution.

Some of these children have exhibited a profound understanding of the function of the Constitution in American society. Witness the following from a first-grader whose piece is included in this volume:

"The Constitution is like a stop sign in the road. The stop sign stops you from bumping other people's cars. This lets everyone drive down the road without getting hurt. The Constitution stops you from bumping into other people's freedoms. This lets everyone live without hurting other people's rights."

I hope all of us will learn much from what these young people have written about the Constitution. The future of our Constitution rests in their hands.

Given the Chief's strong features and shock of white hair, most viewers always perceived him as an austere, sober, elevated man, which he was. But he loved children and was warm and caring around them. He wrote the following letter to young campers:

SUPREME COURT OF THE UNITED STATES
WASHINGTON, D.C. 20543
CHAMBERS OF
CHIEF JUSTICE BURGER
RETIRED
JULY 28, 1989

Dear Campers:

I was a bugler, lifeguard, truck driver, and sometimes cook's helper at Camp St. Croix many, many years ago.

I am now Chairman of the Commission on the Bicentennial of the United States Constitution and my "bugle" is to tell the story of the Constitution.

Cordially,
Chairman

Mark Cannon reports that "When the political pressures of World War II uprooted West Coast Japanese Americans, some were sent to Minnesota. Despite resistance, Warren Burger created a committee to help them and took one family into his home for nearly a year. When we lectured in Tokyo in 1974, a lady came to him for an emotional reunion. She was the two-year-old whose family had found haven in the Burger home." And General Days said, "He was a man who for more than ten years sent pins garnered in his world travels to the handicapped child of a former clerk."

CHAPTER 5

CAPTAIN OF THE SHIP

The Chief ran a tight ship, but he did so to prevent political diversions. The staff was advised always to keep him informed of any requests made by Commissioners. The Chief asked me to write the following memos, one to Congressional aides (which he edited) and one to Commissioner Betty Murphy:

> DECEMBER 19,1989
> MEMORANDUM
> TO: Carolyn Osolinik, Malcolm Richardson
> FROM: Ron Trowbridge
> SUBJECT: Media Advisory Committee
>
> Regarding our suggestion that a Media Advisory Committee meeting be held in January, the Commission staff will of course be happy to provide logistical and other support should Senator Kennedy or Mrs. Cheney wish to call a meeting.
>
> As you know, Chief Justice Burger has frequently emphasized that each committee is and has been free at all times to meet and generate programs and recommendations; at all times programs other than routine implementation have been cleared with relevant committees preceding Commission meetings.
>
> If you will give us the word, we will be pleased to facilitate the meeting as they wish.

MEMORANDUM
TO: BETTY SOUTHARD MURPHY
FROM: RON TROWBRIDGE
SUBJECT: CLEARANCE PROCESS

At a meeting on January 28 with staff Directors, the Chief Justice reminded us that all Commissioners' requests for work or action by staff must be directed by the Commissioners to Mark [Cannon], Staff Director, and not his subordinates. Perhaps the best way to facilitate this would be that when you have requests of Louise, Don or me, that these requests be directed to Mark with a copy simultaneously sent to me. I can then work in conjunction with and clear my actions through Mark. This will generally necessitate your putting requests for work in writing, but it's good to have such in writing anyway for the historical record as well as to help you be assured that we know what you want.

The Chief told me that when he was angry with someone, he would write a sharp rebuke, then put it in his top drawer. He usually wouldn't send it, but the process enabled him to vent his anger and provided a kind of catharsis. One angry letter he did not put into his drawer was to me. It is the only rebuke in writing or verbally that I ever received from him in the nine-plus years I worked for or with him:

January 18, 1989
CONFIDENTIAL
MEMORANDUM FROM THE CHAIRMAN
To: Ron Trowbridge

I am "resigning" as "Staff Director" of the Commission on the Bicentennial as of January 1, even though I have been performing those functions by and large since the beginning. I put it this way in order to make my point that I do not want to continue to be the Staff Director. I was appointed as Chairman and the reason I feel so strongly is that I have been both Chairman and Staff Director, as you well know.

We have had two examples this week of what I want corrected.

(1) I do not want any subject, any proposal, any matter, except in an emergency, presented to me that has not been fully analyzed by the staff and passed by you before it is presented to me. In short, what I want you to do if you are going to be Staff Director is to do just what I have been doing at these staff sessions.

(2) It should have been clear by now from the situation we were confronted with by the "L.B.J. Library Proposal," for example, and several other related matters that the staff must have raw material presented by the proposer. Apparently I failed to get this procedure across, but it will now be understood and acted upon.

In short, you review it before it ever comes to me.

His resignation of micromanagement lasted until—the next day. He cared too much about celebrating the Constitution to do otherwise. He ran too tight a ship and could never bring himself to be anything other than an ubiquitous captain. I could not hold this against him for the obvious reason that he cared dearly about the precious Constitution and was going to make certain that we commemorated its Bicentennial properly. Moreover, he wanted careful control so as to ensure that the Bicentennial was not politicized or made controversial. Ours was to be a history and civics lesson, and he resigned as Chief Justice to achieve this.

But he was not hubristic. He sent me the follow memo:

NOVEMBER 6, 1989
MEMORANDUM FROM THE CHAIRMAN
To: Ron Trowbridge
Re: newsletters

A long time ago I requested that no newsletter have more than one photo (if any) of me.

This current issue has five.

Please hereafter let me see the full copy before printing.

And he edited and paid attention to detail with incredible, painstaking scrutiny. I used to watch with fascination as he would correct a letter I wrote by changing here a single word or there a single word so as to get the nuances just exactly right. He revised letters sometimes over and over again. Figure 3 shows a letter that I wrote to Admiral Hill at the Middle Temple with the Chief's revisions. After I wrote the letter incorporating those revisions, he again revised it, and those revisions are shown in Figure 4. It is well known in Washington that clerks for members of the Supreme Court frequently write decisions for their members. If that, in fact, was the case with Chief Justice Warren Burger, I am certain I can assume that those writings by clerks were always heavily revised or, if not revised, at least every word carefully read and agreed to. It is fair to say that any decision that came forward from the Chief Justice's office did in fact convey precisely the thoughts of the Chief.

In one report I prepared for the Chief, I stated, "I am sending you the following update." The Chief crossed out "update" and wrote this note by hand across the top of the page: "No such word as 'update.' (How about 'downdate'?)" He was traditional not only in ethics but also in word usage.

One of my very worst days at the Commission was the day the Chief ordered me to "fire ten people." I could select any ten I wanted, but because the bulk of the Commission's activities were now over—we had celebrated in 1987 the writing of the Constitution and the Ratification and were now moving on to celebrate the Bill of Rights—we no longer needed the huge staff. As I recall, there were over 100 people on the staff. I was faced with the horrible task of being a draconian Greek messenger. For about a week before the dismissals, I could not sleep. I thought about those people as being married with spouses, with children—what would they do for a living in a town where it is not easy, owing to fierce competition, to get a job? But the Chief was dead right, we did not need those people, ours was not a government welfare program. So on the given day, one by one, I brought the people into the office and announced unfortunately that we no longer needed them. I tried to be as euphemistic as possible. Some met this with acceptance; some were angry as hell. Some were vitriolic; some simply started to cry out loud, with tears streaming down the face and sobs. One woman was sobbing so loudly that she couldn't talk and finally just got up and walked out. As I think back upon that horrible day, then and now, I felt awful; on the other hand, I knew that the Chief was right.

The Chief was always interested in saving money. In fact, he frequently pointed out to Congressional committees that, when he was Chief Justice at the Supreme Court, at the end of the fiscal year he would with joy and pride return government funds to the Treasury. That kind of thing was unheard of in Washington, D.C., where virtually everyone scrambled to make sure all funds were spent by the end of the fiscal year so as not to be punished with reduced funds accordingly in the next year.

With regard to frugality, the Chief wrote a memo of January 19, 1989, to me regarding flawed pocket Constitutions: "The mistaken copies of the pocket Constitution should not be used for any purpose. I suggest that in some way you mark those boxes so that they are not even opened. However, there is a possible use of them that could be a good 'salvage' outside the United States, but put that on the agenda for discussion before we do anything or release a single copy of the mistaken issue." One of the statements we heard from the Chief constantly with regard to projects seeking grants was, "Not one thin dime!" And he sent a memo to me on one grant demanding an accountability of "where every penny is spent." Another memo to me began, "I have noticed on several of the brochures that have been handed to me that we have blank spaces on the opening cover and on the back cover. The basic rule should be never, never, never waste that kind of space."

Now comes an absolutely delightful story about the Chief regarding *no type*

Supreme Court of the United States
Washington, D. C. 20543

Return to Fronkside

CHAMBERS OF
CHIEF JUSTICE BURGER
RETIRED

December 11, 1987

Dear Admiral Hill: *is* (*We hope to draw*) *for one event*

Thank you for ~~the promptness~~ of your November 27th letter. My *tentative*
suggestions ~~are~~ that the number of American speakers be limited
to three, ~~one for each of the three evenings,~~ and that they be
high-level nationally known figures, ~~possibly~~ former Cabinet
members, former Members of Congress ~~or~~ eminent historians, *political*
would also urge that no American names be cited in writing at *scientists.*
this time to avoid premature commitment.
I have thought of this in terms of 3 persons on a panel
You also ~~might want to consider amending the~~ topic ~~for day three~~
~~to~~ include the two-way influence of the British on the American
framers and the influence of our Constitution in England and
elsewhere abroad. Would not such a discussion of your influence
upon us gain a wider audience in England? *said it was not unlike it that* *Could be allowed*

Lord Templeman ~~expressed to me his permission for the~~ BBC to film
the proceedings in the Middle Temple. ~~I~~ had several meetings
with the very top leadership of BBC, who expressed a genuine
interest in cooperating with us on Bicentennial programming.

~~Finally, as to format,~~ Lord Templeman suggested the possibility
of the ~~three Americans~~ submitting papers in advance to British
~~counterparts for response and subsequent discussion.~~ The
audience would ~~be the largest~~, composed of jurists, historians,
lawyers, and the academic community, ~~both~~ faculty and students.
This ~~venue and format~~ would dovetail nicely with your suggestion
that the Law Society, the Royal Institute of International
Affairs, and the International Institute for Strategic Studies be
invited to participate *in the dialogue.*

With season's greetings,

Cordially,

Rear Admiral J. R. Hill
Under Treasurer
The Treasury
Middle Temple
London EC4Y 9AT

on stipulated subjects with advance papers, if possible, to guide moderator,

Figure 3

Supreme Court of the United States
Washington, D. C. 20543

CHAMBERS OF
CHIEF JUSTICE BURGER
RETIRED

from our side.

December 15, 1987

refrain from citing any

Dear Admiral Hill:

Thank you for your November 27th letter. My tentative *thinking* suggestion is that the number of American speakers for one event *[?]* be limited to three, and that they be high-level nationally known figures. We hope to draw on former Cabinet members, former Members of Congress, eminent historians, and political scientists. I would also urge that no American names be cited in writing at this time, to avoid premature commitment.

experience

I have thought of this in terms of three persons on a panel on stipulated subjects, with advance papers, if possible, to guide the moderator. One topic might include the two-way influence of the British on the American framers and the influence of our Constitution in England and elsewhere abroad. Would not such a discussion of your influence upon us gain a wider audience in England? *What of the converse? We also*

Lord Templeman said it was not unlikely that BBC could be allowed to film the proceedings in the Middle Temple. We had several meetings with the very top leadership of BBC, who expressed a genuine interest in cooperating with us on Bicentennial programming.

I assume

The audience would be composed of jurists, historians, lawyers, and the academic community, faculty and students. This would dovetail nicely with your suggestion that the Law Society, the Royal Institute of International Affairs, and the International Institute for Strategic Studies be invited to participate in the dialogue.

As to subjects, the following are "on the table":

(a) Historical background and the setting: political, economic and international
(b) Separation of powers
   - Foreign policy, War Powers Act
   - Domestic, budget
(c) Judicial Review
   (1) Marbury vs. Madison
   (2) Sec. 2, Art, III
   (3) *Challenges to U.S. Sup. court scope of jurisdiction* *(We did not mention BBC.)*

That an open dialogue would follow the principal presentations.

(4) Deference *to political Branches*
   - Snail Darter *case — Tennessee Valley Authority v. Hill 457 U.S. 153 [?]*
   - Federal Reserve *— Dimension Financial*

I hesitate to mention names of possible participants, but I assure you they will be at the highest level.

With season's greetings,

Cordially,

Board of Governors v. Dimension Financial Corp. 106 S. Ct. 681, 474 U.S. 361 (1986).

Rear Admiral J. R. Hill
Under Treasurer
The Treasury
Middle Temple
London EC4Y 9AT
England

Figure 4

frugality. We at the Commission regarded Friday as "cruising day." That was the day the Chief would cruise around the Supreme Court looking for someone to go to lunch with him. About half of the time he was successful, lunching with Lewis Powell or other members of the Court or friends. But when unsuccessful, he would invariably call me. And I always stood ready on Friday in late morning to receive a call from him asking if we could lunch together. Often he came down to staff headquarters, bringing with him *always* the same lunch: turkey club sandwiches from the Supreme Court cafeteria. But on some occasions he wanted to go either to the Lawyer's Club or the City Tavern Club. On one particular day, however, he wanted to do something radically different: go to a restaurant where he could get a cocktail. The Chief rarely drank, though he enjoyed fine wine, but on this day he wanted a drink and asked me if I knew of any place nearby where we could get one. I told him that close by was Baker's, which, being about a block from the White House, served yuppies interested in furthering their careers. When we walked in, practically everyone in the room turned suddenly, tapping one another on the shoulder and pointing to the Chief, who was obviously the kind of celebrity they were looking for in a restaurant like this.

The Chief wanted this time to treat us to drinks, the party consisting of him, one other staffer and myself. Now, a cocktail in Washington, D.C. in those days cost about five dollars. We ordered three cocktails and the Chief gave the waiter ten dollars. About ten minutes later, and I will never forget his exact words, he leaned over to me and said, "Say, Ron, do you suppose he forgot to bring me my change?" "Oh Chief," I said, "inflation is terrible these days and I think the ten dollars covered all three drinks and the tip." He shook his head in disbelief. A few moments later the owner came to our table and thanked the Chief profusely for coming to his restaurant. He was not about to tell the Chief that he owed him another five bucks.

We have to remember that the Chief was a product of the Depression, and we also have to remember that he just did not deal much with money. At the Court, he was always taken care of, chaperoned, hosted and the like, and cocktails were something he rarely paid for. Nor did he carry much money. I recall the day I stood in the foyer at his home, the two of us about to depart for a week in England. His wife Vera said, "Now Warren, be sure to take some money." The Chief responded with some agitation, waving his arms, "Vera, I have money!" He had $100. After two days in London, he asked if I could lend him some money. At the end of the trip, he asked me for another loan so that he could take home some sealed smoked salmon.

There is another wonderful story about the Chief that demonstrates, in my view, the right kind of integrity that he gave to the Office of the Chief Justice of the United States. At first blush, his actions might seem those of an arrogant, hubristic man, but I do not think that is the point at all. The occasion was as follows: After we had performed our moot court cases at Oxford University, the Middle Temple, and University of Dublin, I took him back to Heathrow Airport so that he might take the plane home. He had asked me to remain behind for a day or so to work out arrangements with the BBC and the taping of the moot court cases. I escorted him through Heathrow Airport, taking him as far as I could go. "Chief, the plane is just through that door about fifty feet away," and then I left him. The next day I found out he did not take the plane. It was British Air, and to get on board he was required to go through a magnetometer. He would not do that because he was the former Chief Justice of the United States, which in terms of protocol ranks second only to the President of the United States. Of course, the British official did not know who he was and required that he go through the magnetometer. Rather than do so, he chose to walk out and find the Pan Am terminal, where he was known and therefore would not have to pass through the magnetometer. He sat there for some six hours waiting for the next plane to the United States. Rather than take the one second it would take to walk through the British magnetometer, he chose instead to sit several hours so that he could preserve the integrity of the office.

The same intention operated at Dulles airport. Whenever we flew from that airport, I worked out in advance an arrangement with the manager ensuring that the Chief could bypass magnetometers.

There is also the revealing story the Chief told me of magnetometers and one of his White House visits. President Reagan had invited him to dinner. When one goes to the White House, one must go through magnetometers. The Chief refused to do so. The guards on duty recognized him, but still refused to allow him to bypass the magnetometers. He then told the security guards, "Who's going to tell President Reagan that you would not let me in— you or me?" The guards let him in. His analogy to me was entirely valid: If the President of the United States were to visit the Supreme Court, no one there would dare suggest that he must walk through magnetometers. By the same token, if the Chief Justice of the United States visits the White House, no one should dare to insult that Chief Justice by insisting that he pass through magnetometers. The issue was the integrity of the Office. Fair enough.

On one occasion, he needed to have repaired the 1987 Cadillac Sedan that was lent him from General Motors. On October 2, 1992, the Chief wrote those of us on the private Trust a memo requesting that we pay the service bill of $910.57 for routine maintenance on his Cadillac. In this memo he justified that payment by the following: "Even though somewhere between $60,000 and $75,000 of the assets of the Trust at the present time came from my personal contributions, I prefer to have the trustees act on the payment of the current Lindsey Cadillac bill." The Trust paid the bill, concluding that the Chief had done more than his fair share of work for both the Bicentennial Commission and the Trust. After all, his pay for his duty as Chairman of the Bicentennial Commission was commensurate with the pay the Founding Fathers received—nothing.

Col. O'Meara narrates an embarrassing story about this limousine:

When the Commission first got started, the Chief negotiated with Roger Smith, then CEO of GM, to give him a stretch limousine. And, over the years, that lease (free lease from GM) had to be renegotiated each year. While the Chief felt that the loan was for the life of the Commission, the underlings at General Motors thought that it was only for a year. Their concern, they told me after four years, was that they were in the new car business and not the used car business. But they weren't about to ask Roger Smith what he had agreed to, nor were they going to argue with the Chief as to what the arrangement was, so we got to keep it. The Cadillac was actually licensed to Cadillac Motor Corporation, in the Eastern District in Philadelphia. So any tickets that might result from that went to them. And the Chief habitually took the car home at night, particularly on the weekends, and drove it himself.

On one occasion he was driving it in Arlington and decided to stop at the shopping center, where he parked in a handicapped parking space. Of course, from the Chief's point of view, he was handicapped with a bad back from polio, so he felt he was entitled to park there. But he didn't have the necessary permission. Naturally, he got a ticket. The following Monday morning, the regular driver from the Marshall's office got in the car and found the ticket wadded up on the floor of the limousine. He went to the Chief and asked him about it and asked if he wanted him to take care of the ticket. The Chief said, 'No, just ignore it.' After a month or two passed on that ticket, I got a call from General Motors in Philadelphia wanting to know what the story was on the ticket. There was a fine of $125 that needed to be paid. I discussed it again with the Marshall driver and he indicated that the Chief absolutely refused to have him get involved with the local police about getting a ticket withdrawn. It was left to me to take care of.

I took care of it. But it was a matter of principle from the Chief's point of view. He was handicapped.

Col. O'Meara relates another story, this time amusing, about the Chief's frugality:

> West Point gives out not every year, but on occasion, what they call the Thayer Award. It's a beautiful gold medallion, and they give it to statesmen and public figures who have done well in the eyes of the military. The Chief and his wife were invited up for this award ceremony at West Point. He asked that I also go with him. We went over to Andrews Air Force Base, and a small Army twin propeller aircraft (a C-12) flew us to Newburg, New York. We left at about 11:30 a.m. and got there near 1:00 p.m. We were met by an Army Judge Advocate General Corps Colonel with a van that was going to take us from Newburg up to West Point. When we got off the airplane, Mrs. Burger indicated that she was hungry and so was the Chief, so they wanted to get something to eat. When the Colonel met us, I asked him what the plans were. The Burgers were to get in the van and go directly to the Commandant's house, then to the award parade at West Point. I asked if there was any food involved, and he said, "No." So I said, "Well, we need to stop then en route and get something to eat." This put some degree of fear in the eyes of the Colonel who picked us up because he had a schedule to meet and that didn't include stopping for lunch. The only restaurant in Newburg was a McDonald's. We stopped there, and the minute we arrived he went to the telephone to call and indicate that we were going to be delayed a little.
>
> We walked into McDonald's, and I believe, from the reaction of the Chief, that this was probably the first time he'd ever been in a McDonald's. He obviously remembered, however, that shortly after the Commission was formed, the Commission got together with a number of commercial fast food sponsors—one in particular was McDonald's—who put out tray liners with different vignettes on them describing the Constitution. He immediately went to where the trays were—of course, they were the dirty trays—and began looking for his tray liners celebrating the Constitution. Since this particular constitutional celebration had been done and gone for at least a year or two, there were no tray liners commemorating the Bicentennial.
>
> Anyway, he then asked for a turkey club sandwich, and of course, all

of us know that there is no such thing as a turkey club sandwich at McDonald's. He then looked up on the board and saw the menu and the prices and had a hamburger and a soda and one of their fried pies and french fries. The prices must have impressed him because he bought the lunch for the five of us. As we were sitting, he remarked about how great the hamburgers were and how absolutely delicious the pie was.

Time was getting away from us, and the Colonel from West Point was having a fit. Eventually we left and arrived at the Commandant's house for a brief greeting, then were off to the parade field. On the field was a brigade of the Corps Cadets waiting for the Chief Justice. The Chief was offered a chair to sit on while the brigade passed in review, but the Chief stood tall and stood throughout the entire parade. In my later discussion with the Corps of Cadets, they indicated that they knew that the Chief was going to be late and the reason for it was that he had had a "Big Mac attack" en route from Newburg to West Point.

Why did the Chief Justice resign from the Court in 1986? Probably for a number of reasons. He told me personally that he did not think it necessary for a Supreme Court Justice to stay on until he was carried out feet first. Some Justices had nearly done that. He has also said publicly that he thought at this point in his life he could be replaced as Chief Justice and that the Commission work, given that it was the time of the Bicentennial of the Constitution, was a call whose timing was more important.

And I recall that he actually stated in public that he regarded working for the Commission as being "more important" than being Chief Justice. He denied, to me at least, and to the press I think, that he resigned in order that Reagan during his presidential term might be able to choose his successor. The Chief's successor, Chief Justice William Rehnquist, reported at the memorial tribute:

> When he retired as Chief Justice in 1986, he said that one of the reasons he did so was that he could not do justice to both the office of

Chief Justice and his position as Chairman of the Committee on the Bicentennial of the Constitution.

When asked why he had chosen his Chairmanship over the Chief Justiceship, he replied that he thought the President would have no trouble finding someone to be Chief Justice, but he might have trouble finding someone to be Chairman of the Committee on the Bicentennial. After his retirement, he was able to concentrate on the Bicentennial Commission and bring that tremendous energy to bear to make Americans better acquainted with their Constitution.

Near the end of his life, we were always after the Chief to write his memoirs. He was interested, but I suspect that he just couldn't muster the time nor perhaps the energy to put it all together. He did have a title for his book: "Swift Seasons." He told me he preferred that title because at the end of his life he found that years were moving swifter than they had earlier. I also think that the Chief, though an inordinately private man, might have approved the book that I am writing here because it was in the spirit of "Swift Seasons," that is, an intimate personal reflection about the man.

CHAPTER 6

THE CHIEF'S CONSERVATISM

On the matter of Affirmative Action, racial set asides, and cross-district busing, the Chief volunteered a curious observation to me. He said that blacks, but not Hispanics, Asians, Native Americans or any other group, deserved special treatment for historical reasons. He said that blacks did not originally come to America on their own accord but, rather, were brought in against their will as slaves. Therefore, he argued, they were owed special treatment. He was especially sensitive to matters relating to blacks, and in one memo of November 20, 1989, he wrote,

> We have had some discussion about how to identify the programs for 1991 concerning the Bill of Rights. If we use the title "Bill of Rights," we surely must add something about the subsequent amendments, especially the Civil War Amendments, but not limited to them. I would like to have the Committee consider whether we should develop some other designation such as "Human Rights under the American Constitution."

The Chief's view on blacks was relevant to my exchange with *National Review*. When he died, I wrote *National Review* asking if I could write their obituary on him. They agreed; I sent the following obituary:

Warren Burger: A Profile in Gentlemanly Courage

As Staff Director for the Commission on the Bicentennial of the U.S. Constitution, I had the chance for two years to work daily with "the Chief." Nixon had appointed him Chief Justice solely on the basis of a piece that Burger had written for Ripon magazine. After reading it I told the Chief, "You're a closet liberal"; he smiled, responding, "Tell Ted [Kennedy], but don't tell Phyllis [Schlafly]," who were members of the Bicentennial Commission.

But the Chief was tougher, more principled than most Republican Executive Branch heads when it came to battles with Congress. Congress wanted to confiscate nearly $1 million from the Bicentennial Commission for the Lyndon Johnson Library to write a book exclusively on Congress (not the Executive or Judicial branches), never mind that Congress already had its own branch's budget and staff. The Chief said no. Senator Hollings was then Chairman of the relevant Senate appropriations committee and his staffer called me often in anger and threateningly, "I have never seen such arrogance as the Chief displays . . . . How could he dare defy the Chairman of the Committee; no one does that . . . . *You* tell Burger . . . ." When I reported this back to the Chief, he threatened to resign, saying that he would hold a press conference on the constitutionality of the separation of powers. The Chief held out for about a year, but I knew that eventually Congress would triumph. Finally Senators Hollings and Byrd ganged up on him, declaring that either he would go along cooperatively with Congress or Congress would earmark the funds within the Commission's budget.

When the Bicentennial Commission sought calendar photos reflecting generically each of the three branches of government, Speaker of the House Jim Wright sent over a picture of just himself at the gavel, to the exclusion of the rest of Congress. The Chief chuckled. The more threatening Wright's staff became in demanding the lone pose, the more resolute the Chief's principles. It was such a refreshing change for me in Washington, where I spent nine years, to work for someone with real courage.

Ted Kennedy once called a Bicentennial Commission staff meeting without the knowledge of Chairman Burger. We were to meet, suspiciously, in a hotel away from the staff headquarters that Burger visited daily. I told the Chairman, my boss, who then showed up at Kennedy's clandestine meeting uninvited. He was not about to let any politician steer the Commission in a political direction. And after Senator Kennedy railed against

Judge Bork's nomination, Burger declared publically that Bork was "the best qualified candidate" for the Supreme Court "in the last 50 years."

The Chief demonstrated physical courage, too. Polio in youth left him with a severely deformed spine that caused spasms throughout his life. It was painful for him to stand for any length of time, yet at Hillsdale College's Commencement he was moved to stand for an hour and a half shaking the hand of each of the 233 graduates receiving diplomas. The gentleman, always.

Chief Justice Burger seemed terribly austere and most people were scared to death of him, but I cannot tell you how many times he would cry over such things as third graders reading their essays on what the Constitution meant to them. Virtually anything kids did brought him to tears. He had a great sense of dry humor and could be teased. When I did so, he would point his finger at me as though shooting a gun, smiling. I loved the man. The country has lost a rare Statesman.

There is a final irony in all this. Though he loved being with people, the Chief was an extremely private man. I believe he distanced himself intimately from others because individuals were always seeking his views on Supreme Court decisions and he wanted to protect the integrity of the Court. As a result of his privacy, almost no one visited him in the final months of his life. He died the loneliest man I know.

About a week later, I called *National Review* to see whether having received my piece they would print it as promised. "Yes," they replied. About a week later, I received the following letter:

July 15, 1995

Dear Ron,

You either have seen already or will very shortly see that we didn't after all use your obituary except by reference, and I wanted to explain.

Warren Burger, we realized when we sat down to edit the section, occupied too pivotal a role in our recent history for an evaluation not to be in order. This was precisely not the kind of farewell notice you had written or wanted to write—and yet we didn't have room for both.

I am very sorry, because I know how much his friendship meant to you; but we found that journalistically we just couldn't place the personal over the public in this case.

All best wishes,

National Review then printed in place of mine the following obituary:

Warren Burger, RIP

A case of polio in his youth left Chief Justice Warren Burger with a severely deformed spine that made standing for any length of time painful. Yet as Hillsdale College's Ronald Trowbridge reports, at a commencement a few years ago he stood for an hour and a half shaking the hands of 233 graduates. The gentleman, always.

Warren Burger entered the national arena in 1952, when he moved the Minnesota delegation from Harold Stassen to Dwight Eisenhower at the Republican Convention, putting Ike over the top. His last public service was chairing the Commission on the Bicentennial of the Constitution. But his reputation rests on his tenure as Chief Justice from 1969 to 1986. The Warren Court had been a collective devil figure for conservatives for years. The election of Richard Nixon, followed by a string of judicial appointments, was supposed to change all that. Burger did compare endless death-row appeals to a "sporting contest," and attacked rigid applications of the exclusionary rule as "bizarre." But the Burger Court upheld busing and created the right to abortion. (Chief Justice Burger himself backed away from the latter position, but by then the damage was done.) The model of the Court as an eccentric super-legislature remained unchanged.

When Republicans occupy the White House, they often appoint conservative Justices. Sometimes they stay that way (William Rehnquist, Clarence Thomas). Sometimes they don't (David Souter). Intervening Democrats add a few liberals, and jurisprudence lurches along from case to case.

The only hope for long-range reform is a change in the culture of law schools and law professors, which the Federalist Society hopes to bring about; or a Congress willing to pick a fight on the basis of Article III, Section 2 of the document Warren Burger loved so devotedly, and served so haphazardly.

My guess is that *National Review* felt that it had to attack Burger, especially on the issues of busing and abortion. But some rebuttal was necessary, and I sent the following letter to the editor about NR's obituary, which was printed:

Served the Constitution Well

I thought "Warren Burger, RIP" ["The Week," July 31] evenhanded—except for one phrase, when you referred to his serving the Constitution "so haphazardly." To be sure, he was not as conservative as you or I. As his staff director for the Commission on the Bicentennial of the Constitution I once told him, not entirely in jest, that he was a "closet liberal." But generally what he did, with some sensational exceptions, on the Court and elsewhere, was conservative and compliant with the original intent of the framers of the Constitution.

I once asked Arthur Shenfield, past president of the [libertarian] Mont Pelerin Society, to evaluate Burger as Chief Justice. He said, "B+"—an exceptionally high mark from Arthur, who in constitutional matters was rougher even than Lino Graglia.

Most of the individuals I interviewed for this book ranked the Chief politically at about a six, with one being extremely liberal and ten, extremely conservative. His votes on busing and abortion were chiefly the ones responsible for views of him as a centrist on the Court. Yet as I mentioned earlier, he supported busing because he believed that blacks alone were owed special preference because they were brought to this country unwillingly. And while he voted with the majority on *Roe v. Wade*, he never meant for it to be abortion on demand; he later dissented in writing, and he believed that the Supreme Court ought to rehear the case. In *Roe*, he may well, as Judge Bork suggests, have sided with the majority in order to assign the opinion and limit the damage. Burnett Anderson hinted something of this in our interview.

But in other ways I found the Chief quite conservative or traditional. His remarks at the Osgoode Hall Law School on September 20, 1985, remind us of Edmund Burke or Russell Kirk:

REMARKS OF WARREN E. BURGER
CHIEF JUSTICE OF THE UNITED STATES
AT THE OSGOODE HALL LAW SCHOOL
TORONTO, CANADA
FRIDAY, SEPTEMBER 20, 1985

Two things were utterly unique about this Constitution and what flowed from it. First, its structure with division into three co-equal, co-ordinate branches of government was deliberately created to provide for checks and balances. This had never been tried in all human history. Experience demonstrates that our kind of structure does not necessarily produce the most efficient government, but that it does protect freedoms. Efficiency in the private sector, in the conduct of business and industry is critical, but efficiency was not the primary objective of the draftsmen of the Constitution. Freedom from the kind of restraints, which brought people from Europe to this continent, was the primary objective.

The second factor is perhaps even more important, but is, in a sense, a project of the first. The freedom created by this new system unleashed the energies, abilities and talents of every individual to develop as the individual's own ambitions, abilities and industry allowed. In the short space of 200 years, this small contingent of three-million people, scattered along the eastern seaboard, developed into a country of 250 million and a world power. Other nations had industrious, talented and ambitious people, but the uniqueness here was that this new system allowed every person to develop God-given talents and abilities without the heavy hand of government or tradition being a barrier or burden. This theme, which we share with the people of Canada, must be expanded and repeated constantly over the next few years as we celebrate this great experiment in government.

The delegates left Philadelphia exhausted but rightly entitled to be elated, but the document they produced had yet to run the gauntlet of the states' ratification processes and receive the approval of nine states.

We have survived and prospered for 200 years because our strength was not simply in the concepts of the Declaration and the Constitution—great as they are—but because of the strength of the people, of personal integrity, of individual responsibility, of the traditions of home and family—and of a firm belief that our Constitution, as James Madison said, was divinely inspired.

Similarly, his former clerk Ken Starr said of him:

This gracious sensitivity was manifested in his commitment to the concept of ordered liberty . . . including a generous regard for the importance of basic human liberty. Statist impulses, he believed, needed to be curbed when they ran afoul of clearly protected constitutional interests. Especially poignant was his treatment of the right of religious minorities to carry on their own lives free of regulation that failed to satisfy the most urgent needs and demands of organized society. His very moving description in *Wisconsin v. Yoder* of life among the Amish community and the need more broadly to preserve deeply held non-majoritarian values, as against the power of the secular state, stands as an eloquent tribute to fundamental constitutional norms.

Born early in a Century remarkable for both its progress and its horror, Chief Justice Burger, as those of us privileged to serve him know, never succumbed to moral diseases that have so beplagued what Paul Johnson has called simply "modern times." The old and enduring values and virtues, like old time religion, were good enough for the Chief. Not that they simply were of great vintage, but that they were, in his considered judgment, right and good. They were, as T.S. Eliot said, "the permanent things."

Moreover, the Chief's comments on December 14, 1989, for the preface of a version of the Constitution for Eastern Europe were quite traditional:

EASTERN EUROPE
DATE TYPED: DECEMBER 14, 1989
DRAFT

Ever since people came out of caves and joined with others in tribes and towns and villages they have had to balance order with liberty. Freedom had to be balanced with the need for security and with the balance favoring freedom. The delegates who wrote this Constitution in Philadelphia in 1787 did not invent all the ideas and ideals it embraced but drew on the wisdom of the ages to combine the best of the past into a new conception of government: rule by the people with limits on government to protect freedom.

It was not perfect; it is not perfect today even with amendments, but it has continued longer than any other system under a written Constitution. It drew on the Declaration of Independence of 1776 which expressed people's ageless yearning for freedom. It was the beginning of fulfillment of the promises of the Declaration of 1776. People were meant to be free to develop talents given by their Creator.

This Constitution creates three separate, independent branches of government, the checks and balances that keep the total government within the boundaries set by the organic law. The Constitution is the whole and is superior to the parts. It does not always produce tidy results; it depends on the clash of plurality views as to what is best for all; it rests on bargaining and compromise. It has worked for 200 years to unleash the energies and talents of people to create a good life.

The whole system rests on the first three words, WE THE PEOPLE, and what follows divides and delegates the powers but powers that are harnessed and limited to preserve liberty with order.

CHAPTER 7

COURAGEOUS BATTLES
WITH GOVERNMENT

The Chief was willing to wage principled battles against the branches of government.

A number of public and private organizations approached the Bicentennial Commission seeking Official Recognition for their public or private Bicentennial programs. One such application came from the National Park Service of the Department of Interior for a drama called *Four Little Pages*—a reference to the four original pages of the Constitution. There were, however, some problems with this play, and the Chief was quite happy to grant recognition provided these problems were worked out. So an exchange took place between David Dame of the Park Service and me; I sent the following memo under my signature to Dame—it was written entirely by Chief Justice Burger:

> TO: David Dame
> FROM: Ron Trowbridge
> SUBJECT: *Four Little Pages*
> DATE: July 31, 1986
>
> Per our phone discussion today I am sending you the comments (below) on the play from our Education division. Let's stay in on-going touch in the hope of working this matter out smoothly. Please do get back to me as soon as you've had a chance to act at your end. Thanks.
>
> I would recommend some changes on page 19. Unless it can be verified that Franklin said, "its [the Constitution's] very imperfections

are what make it hold up," I would delete this. If there are characteristics which contribute to the Constitution's lasting 200 years, they should not be called imperfections. In this same speech, instead of ". . . it bends to the needs of the time," I would say "its principles can be applied to problems as they arise."

On page 12, the reference on the nineteen slaveholders is out of place in a list of the offices that the delegates had held. Either the delegates are being listed according to their property holdings or according to their training and experience.

Also on page 12, it mentions that there were no poor men represented—even though some of the delegates had been poor and others later became so—no free blacks—even though there were no unfree blacks, either—and so on. This reflects a basic confusion: the Convention was not a representative body, and did not have, as such, any authority (cf. *Federalist 40*). The exercise of the constituent power belongs to the whole people who were able to vote on the Constitution's adoption. The exercise of the legislative power arguably requires a representation of every group (but, cf. *Federalist 35*); the purely recommendatory "powers" of the Constitutional Convention do not require such "representativeness," and the Convention should not be held to a contemporary standard for legislatures.

On pages 13A, 14 and 15, there are several errors concerning the subject of "The Great Compromise." It settled the question of the basis of representation in Congress, and not questions raised on these pages relative to slavery, the judiciary, and a strong executive.

On page 19. Instead of "there's lots of flaws in these four little pages," I would prefer "and there are some flaws in these four little pages." As the script stands here, it assumes a flawed Constitution. Why state that when earlier it is properly called "the longest running Constitution in world history"?

David Dame responded to my memo, that is, the Chief's memo, as follows, forwarding the Chief Historian's rebuttal:

UNITED STATES DEPARTMENT OF THE INTERIOR
NATIONAL PARK SERVICE
MEMORANDUM
To: Dave Dame, Visitor Service Division
From: Chief Historian
Subject: *Four Little Pages*

We react to Ron Trowbridge's comments on the subject play as follows:

- p. 19, regarding the "imperfections." We begrudgingly come down in favor of Trowbridge's deletion and modified wording, because on balance we believe it expresses Franklin's feelings somewhat better.

- p. 12, referring to the "19 slaveholders." The author is certainly entitled to refer to this fact somewhere in the text. It is fundamental to understanding some of the key debates of the Convention. It may be worked in less awkwardly somewhere else, but we do not agree with deleting it.

- p. 12 in regard to "poor men, free blacks, etc." We believe that it is important for the public to know the types of people who were not present at the Convention. While the character of the Convention can be judged too harshly against the democratic standards of present-day America, the contrast presented makes it clear that we have made progress in 200 years. Trowbridge's attempts to draw a distinction between the Convention and legislatures ignores the fact that the legislatures of 1787 were arguably no more representative than the Convention itself.

- pp. 13a, 14, and 15. The authors should clarify the subject of the Great Compromise. This can likely be done in a single sentence. On the other hand, the cacophonous refrain of suggestions that follows does capture the confused spirit of the debates in the Convention, and should be retained.

- p. 19, regarding "lots of flaws." Likely no one of the framers was completely satisfied with the document, and some, including Franklin in his speech moving the adoption of the Constitu-

tion by the Convention, were very overt in stating their objec-
tions, and then going along in the interests of getting an improved system even with flaws. It seems to us that the "lots of
flaws" refrain is used rhetorically. Franklin is then summoned
to show how the document has lasted 200 years. We think
Trowbridge is being unduly sensitive.

How ironic it is that Mr. Dame's Chief Historian in effect judged the
former Chief Justice of the United States to be "unduly sensitive" about the
Constitution! The matter was finally resolved by compromise, the Commission granting official recognition of the drama.

On June 21, 1989, he transcribed and sent to me a copy of his working
draft entitled, "The Right to Keep and Bear Arms." It stated in rough draft
his position on gun control, the historical setting he thought governed the
issue and how he thought the framers intended the Second Amendment. I
reproduce here the entire rough draft as he edited it (Figure 5).

I had unfathomed respect for the Chief for his independence, courage,
and allegiance to the notion of an independent judiciary and the constitutional separation of powers. He took the separation seriously—and whenever members of Congress tried to muddy the separation of powers, he
recoiled and properly so. He received the following letter from Ernest
Hollings, Chairman of the Commerce, Justice, State, the Judiciary, and
Related Agencies Subcommittee, which was cosigned by Senator Warren
Rudman, Ranking Minority Member:

September 20, 1988

Dear Mr. Chief Justice:
    We were surprised and concerned to learn earlier today of the re-
sponse to the request of Senate Appropriations Committee staff for information relating to the level of unobligated balances available to the Com-

mission on the Bicentennial. As you know, in order for the Appropriations Committee to perform its function, it regularly and routinely asks
for and receives information on the status of the programs it funds. In
this, as in other matters, the staff acts with full authority of the Subcommittee Chairman and Ranking Minority Member.

We would appreciate your directing the staff of the Commission on
the Bicentennial to immediately release information on the level of funds
which have to date been legally obligated. We would anticipate receiving
this information by the close of business Wednesday, September 21, 1988
[the next day].

Thank you for your cooperation in this matter.

The Chief was not about to be unfairly intimidated and fired back the
following response that began:

September 21, 1988

Dear Senator Hollings and Senator Rudman:
I have your letter of September 20, which I received at 6:00 p.m. I
confess a great deal of surprise at its contents, for only last week, on
September 14, I asked for an opportunity to come up and meet with your
staffs, and with you if you were available, or to meet in my Chambers to
discuss the very subject of your letter. My suggestion was rejected. In
short, if you are "surprised," I am also "surprised."

Once again, the right hand did not know what some of the other hands
were doing.

When I served at a high-level position in the Reagan Administration, I
had not experienced Reagan leaders who had the courage to rebut powerful
Senators the way the Chief did. Generally, they acquiesced and would
never dare to think of criticizing those Senators whose committees autho-
rized or provided appropriations. Separation of powers, after all, meant to
the Chief that the Legislative Branch should legislate and the Executive

Return to West

Transcribed: June 21, 1989

The Right to Keep and Bear Arms

Through the efforts of a well-funded, special interest lobby considerable confusion has resulted as to the meaning of the Second Amendment guaranteeing, "the right of the people to keep and bear arms ..." To understand the meaning of this Amendment we must look at the setting in which it was adopted nearly 200 years ago. A very large proportion of the 3 million people living within the 13 original colonies depended upon wild game and a good many of them required fire arms Before the defense from marauding Indians and even from lawless white people.

Even more important was the hostility of Americans toward the idea of standing armies, and the thirteen independent, sovereign states under the Articles of Confederation had no standing army. From the time of the Declaration of Independence through the victory at Yorktown in 1781, George Washington as the field commander-in-chief of all the armies had to depend upon the states and state militia to send volunteers. The victory at Yorktown and subsequently the adoption and ratification of the Constitution did not change people's attitudes about a national army or a standing army. They had lived for years under the notion that each state would maintain its own military establishment. Many of these people and their fathers and grandfathers before them remembered how autocracy was maintained in Europe by means of standing armies controlled by the monarch. Americans wanted no part of this. When the Bill of Rights was adopted in 1791 it is

Figure 5a

- 2 -   *close as the four freedoms of the First Amendment*

interesting to see that this hostility toward a national army or
a standing army, along with the prohibition against quartering
soldiers in a private home, emerged in Amendments II and III. *the People*
understood the need for a militia for a combination of reasons,
given their experience with French and Indian wars and the
marauding Indians and the need on almost a daily basis to go
hunting for wild game as part of the food supply. *A rifle and powder horn were like automobiles in terms of need.*

It was not surprising, therefore, that the relevant
provision concerning arms emerged in very simple terms with the
predicate of the need for *the* well regulated militia. *"ia" of Article II* In less than
three lines the Second Amendment was declared "a well regulated
militia *being* necessary for the security of a free state, the right of
the people to keep and bear arms shall not be infringed." In
the two centuries ~~nearly 200 years~~ since then it has become clear, *sadly,* that ~~no~~ nation *must maintain* ~~can survive without~~ standing military force and, in general, the
military establishment *are* vastly ~~so~~ beyond any conception of that
early day. We still have the "militia" in a sense by way of the
National Guard which can be swiftly integrated into the national
defense forces in time of emergency or war.

The chief controversy *on guns* in our time has ~~not~~ *little* to do with the
of "we the people" "right to bear arms," but the right ~~to buy and own hand guns~~ *through our elected representatives to regulate the purchase and ownership of arms* *including me* ~~without any~~ inquiry ~~into the purpose, without any inquiry~~ into
the background of the purchaser, ~~and without any showing of need.~~
Two hundred years ago *on Madison's proposed Bill of Rights* In the debate in Congress Elridge Gerry, addressing the questions
of the Second Amendment, stated that a militia was necessary, "to

- 3 -

prevent the establishment of a standing army, the bane of liberty...
.... Whenever governments mean to invade the rights and
liberties of the people, they always attempt to destroy the
militia in order to raise an army of their ruins." ~~{~~ annals of
Congress, 749.~~}~~ Clear the historical evidence reveals that the
central purpose of the Second Amendment was to provide for the
"common defense." Of course, the special interest groups would
respond to this by saying that the common defense embraces also
the right of the individual to defend his home; ~~and no one would~~ we need not
challenge that. No one would seriously question that the
Constitution protects the right of hunters to own and keep
shotguns and rifles for hunting game any more than anyone would
challenge the right to own and keep fishing rods and other *The major difference here is that fishing equip^m*
equipment for fishing; ~~But even here there is a marked change in~~
And, for the most part,
~~the sense that~~ hunting today is a recreational activity and not
an imperative of survival. *does not pose massive danger to others.*

The public discussion and debate has been deliberately
clouded by special interest advocates financed to a substantial
extent by the arms industry and the ammunition industry; of that
the scope of the
there can be no doubt. The real question is ~~what~~ right ~~the of~~ *the*
states ~~have~~ to regulate the purchasing and owning of firearms.
To take an extreme case it might be argued under what the special
interest groups have been telling us that the right to own an 18
like the Iowa
inch cannon of the type that is carried on *a* super battle ship, is
embraced within the Second Amendment.

In 1819 (?) The Supreme Court decided That
under the Commerce Clause Congress had the
authority to regulate navigation although
T

Figure 5c

That clause —
Even though the Constitution does not mention
automobiles
The right to own an automobile or ~~a~~ *any* mot*o*r-powered vehicle
including a motor cycle is beyond question, but equally beyond
question is the right of the state*s* to regulate the purchase or
the assignment and transfer of such vehicles and the right to
license the use of those with reasonable standards. In ~~most~~ *many*
even
places, a bicycle must be registered, as must the household dog; *In som*
places
~~And~~ unlicensed dogs may be picked up and destroyed. *of the "rights to bear arms" ?*

be
What then ~~would~~ ,reasonable regulation ~~be ? I suggest that~~ *Woods* it
, it *on*
Would be ~~wholly~~ reasonable for a state to provide that, in order
arm
to ~~own or acquire~~ a fire ~~arm of any kind~~, an application must be
age, residence, employment and
made reciting ~~any~~ prior criminal convictions ~~,along with such~~
~~routine matters as age, place of residence~~, and place of
It
employment. ~~It~~ *Would* ~~not~~ be unreasonable to require that this
application lie on the table for ten days before the license
would be issued? And when the owner of the fire arm decides to
Would , it be Unreasonable that
give or sell the fire arm to another person, the transfer be made
?
essentially as a motor vehicle is transferred today. There is
nothing uncommon of having a driver's license having the
photograph of the licensed person, and that would not seem
unreasonable with respect to fire arms, especially if it were
Would it be Unreasonable too
limited to hand guns. ~~If~~ the state required the fingerprints of
?
the owner or the transferee? ~~that would, undoubtedly, be~~
~~challenged; its reasonableness would have to be established.~~

Figure 5d

Branch execute. But of course, Congress too often wanted to micromanage everything; I found this out from experience, working daily with Congress for nine years, from 1981 to 1990.

Senator James Exon also took on the Chief, only to have his ears boxed:

UNITED STATES SENATE
NOVEMBER 13, 1989
The Honorable Warren E. Burger
Chief Justice
Chairman,
Commission on the Bicentennial of the United States Constitution

Dear Mr. Chief Justice:

Attached is a letter I received from [an organization], a firm located in Lincoln, Nebraska, regarding its difficulty in collecting money due and owing from the Commission on the Bicentennial of the United States Constitution.

I regret that I have to bring this matter to your attention, but it seems, from information available to me, that bureaucratic bungling is rapidly pushing this matter toward time-consuming and costly litigation. Given the facts of this case, it seems that the matter might be quickly resolved with simple good faith discussion between all affected parties.

I would appreciate it if this matter could be looked into, and, if at all possible, a resolution be expedited.

I am told that non-payment of this significant bill is placing [the organization], a company of 27 years, in financial difficulty. A timely resolution of this matter will serve the interest of all involved.

With best wishes.
Cordially,

The Chief responded, setting the record straight in no uncertain terms:

November 29, 1989

Dear Senator Exon:

I have your letter dated November 13, 1989, concerning the [organization] of Lincoln, Nebraska. It appears from the statements contained in your letter that you have not been accurately apprised of the facts in this matter.

The delay to which you refer resulted from a request by the [organization] for an investigation by the Inspector General of the Department of Justice. That request has taken this matter out of the normal audit resolution process.

Yesterday, we received a copy of the final report of the Inspector General, which is enclosed. This report covers a 5-month period and indicates that substantial amounts of federal funds were not used for appropriate grant purposes. The amount of questioned costs ($116,095) greatly exceeds the amount withheld from the cooperative agreement by the government. The Inspector General did not find any "bureaucratic bungling" by the Commission or the Office of Justice Programs. The Commission does not owe any money to the [organization].

We intend to move expeditiously into resolution of audit costs in accordance with applicable government regulations and policies.

Cordially,

The Chief also, in principle , took on the Executive Branch. I wrote congratulating him for reducing an auditor's fee by 50 percent. He responded:

February 10, 1992

Dear Ron:

Many thanks for your letter. I must add that on the [auditor] matter, I wrote a very strong letter to Mr. Darman, pointing out—by inference—that they were a little at fault by making sweeping legislation on audits, without pointing out that application might be made for exclusions.

I am enclosing a copy of that letter as a matter of interest to you. I do not regard the settlement of 50 percent as much of a success, because what was necessary to be done should not have been over $500 to $600, or $1,000 at the outside.

We look forward to seeing you.

Sincerely,

His letter to Richard Darman, Director of the Office of Management and Budget, follows:

January 8, 1992

Dear Mr. Darman:

We have just gone through an extraordinary experience with the audit of the Trust for the Bicentennial of the United States Constitution. In 1990 the Commission entered into a Cooperative Agreement with the Trust, a non-profit corporation, for the production of the Four Presidents Project under the close supervision of the Commission. The grant for $1,365,963 was primarily to cover the cost of a contract with an outside producer which was $1,298,000.

During 1990 the Trust had one employee and issued 27 checks. Under OMB Circular A133, it appeared that the Trust was required to have a full compliance audit. The cost of this audit was $12,027 which the auditors said was a 40% discount on their normal rates.

When we questioned this amount the auditors admitted that the review of expenditures to ensure that government funds were properly expended took only about one day of the 23 days spent meeting the OMB requirements, none of which had any relevance to the Trust's situation.

It seemed incredible to me, based on three years of work in accounting before entering the practice of law, to expect any grant of this nature and magnitude to meet these regulations. Therefore, we request an exemption from these regulations for the remainder of the Four Presidents Project grant to the Trust, which is completed except for resolution of the audit fees. We terminated all audit arrangements with [the auditor] and we declined to pay $12,000 for the audit of 27 checks because this was no more than three to five hours work, except for the demands of OMB Circular A-133.

I will be glad to discuss this subject with your staff.

Cordially,

But there was one battle with Congress that I knew, based on my repeated experiences at USIA, the Chief would eventually lose, but he fought it admirably long. The Bicentennial Commission was funded to celebrate all three branches of government and not treat any one branch with favoritism. Yet, on May 6, 1988, Senator Robert C. Byrd, Chairman of the Bicentennial of the U.S. Senate and Lindy (Mrs. Hale) Boggs, Chairman of the Commission on the Bicentenary of the U.S. House of Representatives, wrote Chief Justice Burger requesting $790,000 from the Commission for an Encyclopedia of Congress, and $109,250 for a First Federal Congress Exhibit at the National Portrait Gallery. Congress had its own funds to celebrate the Bicentennial, but wanted ours (the Commission's) too. No other branch of government made this singular kind of micromanaging request of the Commission.

The Chief responded with proper defiance to this letter on May 12, 1988:

SUPREME COURT OF THE UNITED STATES
WASHINGTON, D.C. 20543
MAY 12, 1988

Dear Senator Byrd:

I acknowledge your letter of May 6th with respect to the suggestion that the Commission on the Bicentennial make a grant of $790,000 for the Encyclopedia of Congress being prepared by the Lyndon B. Johnson Library at the University of Texas, and the suggested grant for $109,250 for part of the cost of an exhibit being planned for the Smithsonian Institution.

You, of course, are familiar with the strictures of the budget of the Bicentennial Commission. I have taken the position that each of the branches of government should sustain its own Bicentennial celebration. We have done that very definitely with the Judicial Branch. We are cooperating with the Bicentennial Committee of the Judicial Conference, and, indeed, that Committee has been a substantial help to us in a way of bearing expenses of projects which are jointly sponsored . . . .

If the Commission were to approve grants in the dimensions described in your letter we would find it difficult, if not impossible, to decline requests in similar dimensions from the Executive Branch and the Judicial Branch, but we have made no grants to Executive or Judicial Branch projects. I am leaving the city, and I will be gone about five days on a Bicentennial program but I will be available to discuss this with you on my return.

Cordially,

As Staff Director reporting directly to the Chief, I began receiving threatening calls from staffers on the Hill, demanding that we fund these projects. An aide to Senator Hollings called me angrily, saying, "You tell Burger . . . ," adding that he had never seen such "insolence" as the Chief's and informing me that no one had ever had the temerity to turn down a funding request from Chairman Hollings. We were threatened that if we did not fund the project, Congress would simply earmark the money, but they preferred that we'd cooperate with Congress. They would micromanage our funds, and it was because of this violation of separation of powers that the Chief threaten to resign from the Commission. He did not approve of special treatment to one branch over the other two.

The Chief courageously resisted for several months, and on November 3, 1988, wrote the following memo to the Commission:

NOVEMBER 3, 1988
MEMORANDUM FROM THE CHAIRMAN
To: Commission on the Bicentennial
Re: Encyclopedia of Congress

The episode of the Conference Report on our budget brought into focus the L.B.J. Library request six months ago for $790,000 to prepare to publish an "Encyclopedia of Congress." The material which I sent you earlier this week concerning our drastic budget cut ($4.5 million) is, I think, related to the letter from the L.B.J. Library. I can't believe anyone would rationally think we should hand out $790,000 on that kind of a showing.

As I indicated in my earlier memorandum, I called for the files on this subject and found that they were very, very scanty—to put it mildly. There is a letter from a Mr. Middleton and some figures on a sheet attached to it, indicating that it was estimated that $661,200 would be used for "staff salaries" and $100,000 for "honoraria." This letter from Mr. Middleton was addressed to me at the Jackson Place headquarters and just when it first came to my attention I am not too certain. There was a standing order that all such letters were to be acknowledged promptly and then, if they seemed to warrant a staffing out, that was to be done.

There is nothing in the file to indicate that this letter and the request was ever staffed out. It now comes into focus because those interested in the L.B.J. Library Project have brought the subject to the Appropriations Committees—realistically—brought pressure to bear where it counts.

The material from the L.B.J. Library is, in the staff's view, utterly inadequate to warrant any more consideration than has been given to it, which concededly has been not very much. I agree. There is no indication anywhere in any material we have received as to what will be the content or on what information the draftsmen of this encyclopedia will rely or what may be the qualifications of the drafters for this important task.

Of course, an adequate Encyclopedia of Congress would be a useful document if there is not one now available. Whether there is any such resource material now in existence I have no idea. But if someone is proposing to spend nearly a million dollars to produce such a book, they have the burden of proof to make a substantial showing of (a) the qualifications of the proposer; (b) the scope and content of the work; and (c) the need for the book. If the proposers can submit an appropriately documented request, it will certainly merit the attention of the Bicentennial Commission.

This issue is especially important in light of the budget cut, made without adequate understanding of the Commission's need for "no year" money so we can plan ahead and have funds for new, unanticipated programs.

For example, we should be free to have a 1989 High School Essay Contest on some subject relating to the formation of the first two branches of the new government. We should have certainty of resources for execution of planning for the Bill of Rights and the Amendments. Perhaps some notice should be taken in 1989 of the creation of the Judiciary Branch and, in 1990, of the advent of the Supreme Court. However, on these two matters, the Judicial Conference Committee on the Bicentennial of the Constitution has an independent budget. (When Columbia University asked for a substantial grant to complete the papers of Chief Justice John Jay, I referred them to that Committee; they made the grant.)

Our kind of Project needs "elbow room" to plan. We are now considerably restricted.

Congress had its own money but it wanted more, and since it controlled the purse strings I knew that it would ultimately triumph, which it did. But the Chief fought a long, courageous and principled battle. Finally he was ganged up on by Senators Hollings, Byrd, Lindy Boggs and others, and he had no choice but to give Congress what it after all could take from him anyhow. It was but one more sad story of how Congress micromanages the Executive Branch and just one more reason why ultimately I would resign, owing to this daily micromanagement.

Then, finally, just six short days after the Chief's memo to the Commission requesting "elbow room" from Congress, Congress lowered the boom in the form of a letter from Lindy Boggs to "Warren," from which I here quote selectively:

CONGRESS OF THE UNITED STATES
HOUSE OF REPRESENTATIVES
WASHINGTON, DC 20515-1802
NOVEMBER 9, 1988
Honorable Warren E. Burger
Chairman
Commission on the Bicentennial of the U.S. Constitution

Dear Warren:

Since I will be out of the Country and unable to attend the meeting of the Finance and Executive Committees scheduled for November 19, I am sending you this letter on the Encyclopedia of Congress project to reaffirm my strong support for it and to clarify any misunderstandings that may have developed regarding it. I am sending the same information to all Commissioners.

[She then gave a lengthy account of the history and value of the project, before dropping the punch line:]

The House conferees preferred not to earmark Commission funds for the Encyclopedia of Congress Project even though they recognized it as a worthy project. The House position prevailed in conference. It is clear, however, that both the House and the Senate expect the proposal to be brought before the full Commission for a vote before November 30.

Lindy Boggs was an absolutely lovely, kind person, and the heavy handedness in her letter was entirely out of character. It was not the Lindy I knew. I want to believe that by virtue of her position as Chairman of the Bicentenary for the House, she was pressured to write such a coercive letter to her friend Warren.

In reflecting upon the Chief's courageous, principled resistence, I was reminded of the wonderful quotation by C. S. Lewis:

Courage is not simply *one* of the virtues, but the form of every virtue at the testing point, which means, at the point of highest reality. A chastity or honesty or mercy which yields to danger will be chaste or honest or merciful only on conditions. Pilate was merciful till it became risky.

CHAPTER 8

THE INAUGURAL FLOAT

One of my fondest memories of the Bicentennial Commission and working with the Chief involved activities surrounding President Bush's Inaugural Parade. The Chief wanted in it a Constitutional float with George Washington riding atop. I was to be George Washington, and the float was to look like an un-scrolled Constitution. The Chief wanted George Washington to wear inside his jacket two huge patches that said, "Made in America." This was to be a double entendre, indicating that both the suit and the Constitution were made in America. As I rode down Pennsylvania on top of the float, I continuously flashed open my vest so that the thousands of people lining the street could see my patch "Made in America." The crowd went wild. They acted like the Americans celebrating the U.S. Olympic Hockey Team's victory over Russia, shouting, "U – S – A! U – S – A!"

George Washington had chosen deliberately to have his inaugural suit designed with American fabric and made in America. He chose this rather than the customary British fabric theretofore used for high-level ceremonies. The Chief wanted my Washington suit to be an exact replication of Washington's Inaugural suit, so I was sent to Williamsburg, fitted there and clothed in a suit identical to Washington's in color, texture and design. The Chief persuaded the Crafted With Pride in U.S.A. Council, Inc. to sponsor the float. The Chief, who was a painter and sculptor, scribbled on sheets of paper what the float would look like, and sent me a memo describing it:

DECEMBER 5, 1988
MEMORANDUM FROM THE CHAIRMAN
To: Ron Trowbridge
RE: Float for Inaugural parade

I am enclosing a rough sketch of what might conceivably be a float for the Inaugural Parade. We haven't got our foot in the door on that as of yet, but let's put this high on the agenda and have somebody immediately, repeat immediately, check with float makers and find out what it would cost to make a float of this kind. The scroll should probably be about seven or eight feet high and could be probably canvas, a fine woven canvas of an amber color. It wouldn't be much trouble to get a local scribner to do the first part of the Constitution on one side and possibly the Bill of Rights on the other or maybe just "We the People" on both sides.

The rest of the float could well be someone from each of the 12 states represented at the Constitutional Convention. At the same time we must consider the situation of Rhode Island and see whether there will be any reaction from that state. However, we have a good defense; Rhode Island just wasn't there.

Let's get the figures first and worry about the details of the materials second.

The Chief wanted our float widely viewed, so he wrote the following letter to Peter Jennings, David Brinkley, Barbara Walters, Tom Brokaw, John Chancellor, Willard Scott, Jane Pauley, Connie Chung, Dan Rather, Ed Bradley, Brian Lamb, and Ted Turner:

JANUARY 17, 1989

Dear Peter Jennings,

The "We the People" Float of the Bicentennial Commission in the January 20 parade will exemplify the five year (1987-1991) Constitutional Bicentennial program and I hope it will catch your eye—and voice!

The live George Washington on the float will be making the central point that our country was the first to have a Constitution emanating from *the people*—not handed down as with Magna Carta. Hence "We the People" will be a constant theme.

But the float will make two points, the second stimulated by George Washington himself 200 years ago in his deliberate effort to promote American industry generally and the textile industry in particular.

To do this, he rejected suggestions that he wear his full dress military uniform at the inaugural and had a suit made from a material fabricated in Connecticut. He could not go to Brooks Brothers or Raleigh's store and buy something off the rack.

To his comrade in arms, General Knox, he wrote asking for some "superfine American broadcloths . . . enough to make me a suit of clothes." Later Washington wrote the Connecticut maker saying: "I shall always take peculiar pleasure in giving every proper encouragement in my power to the manufacturers of my Country."

A news account at the time described the suit as of "so fine fabric, and so handsomely finished, that it was universally mistaken for a foreign manufactured superfine cloth . . . flattering to our own manufacture . . . a distinguished token of attention to the manufacturing interests of our country."

The suit you will see on George Washington (worn by Ronald Trowbridge of the Commission staff) is decorated with brass buttons embossed with an American Eagle design. The material for this suit was provided by "CRAFTED WITH PRIDE IN U.S.A. COUNCIL, INC." and crafted by the Colonial Williamsburg staff. It is a precise copy of Washington's original suit which is now in the custody of the U.S. Park Service.

Some may see a relationship between the focus on "Made in the USA" and the pending disagreement we have with some other countries, as we see our modern George Washington open his coat revealing "Made in the USA." As he points to the facsimile of the opening page of the Constitution, our George Washington will also be emphasizing that this great new concept of government was "made in the USA."

Cordially,

After the parade, the Chief wrote Daniel Frierson of the American Textile Manufacturing Institute, Inc., "You perhaps saw the Bicentennial float on January 20. I heard many comments that it was the most meaningful float in the parade."

The parade had final poignancy for me: As I stood atop the float waiting in line for the parade to commence, I saw President Reagan's helicopter rise above the White House for the last time, circle the Capitol and the Mall, and then depart forever. As I had worked with President Reagan, it was a sad moment.

Chapter 9

The "Four Presidents Project"

The Chief was extraordinarily knowledgeable about the history of the Constitution and the founding fathers. As a child he had polio and was confined to bed for a long time, during which he voraciously read American history. This interest ultimately manifested itself into what the Chief called the "Four Presidents Project."

On October 12, 1989, the Chief sent me the following "working draft" of the "Presidency Project," from which I here quote selectively:

> At present, we have four living past presidents [Nixon, Ford, Carter, Reagan] all active and in good health. Sometime ago it occurred to me that it would be a very useful historical and educational step to have these four men separately interviewed for probably one hour each by a qualified interviewer on their views and conclusions about the institution of the presidency. This would not mean a discussion of particular actions or decisions taken by any one of these past presidents unless they, on their own, wished to discuss those events and decisions. Intermittently, for the past two months, I have talked to probably a dozen people in the aggregate, three of them experts and experienced in the matters of televisions and television production. I have also discussed it with historians and political scientists and the conclusion is unanimous that it would be a very important contribution to the Bicentennial of the Constitution and to history if we could arrange such programs.
>
> I first saw President Carter in Atlanta while I was there for a seminar for the American Academy of Political Scientists. He readily agreed to take part. I next arranged with President Nixon for an appointment and Herbert Brownell and I went to see him at his home in New Jersey. He readily agreed. The next call was to President Ford by phone and he

immediately agreed and the same occurred just a few days ago with President Reagan . . . .

[O]ne of the first steps must be to have a qualified person develop a memorandum with the points to be covered in such interviews so that each past president can be giving the matter some thought and looking at any records they think are relevant. None of the discussions were very specific, but in general I outlined that the interview would be at a place and time convenient to the past presidents and that the interviewer would have to be someone acceptable to the past presidents. The interview would be under the most rigid restrictions we could devise as to just what is the purpose of this enterprise and with great emphasis that it is not a show business but an important historical document. Of course, many names were volunteered as to the interviewer or interviewers and I have tried to brush that off so that there isn't some loose discussion about it. Ron Trowbridge has repeated several times that I should be one of the interviewers but I seriously question that for a number of reasons. First, there is working in the background the matter of separation of powers even though I am no longer in active service. But even more important is the fact that I am not experienced in that kind of a process even though it is not unlike the process of examining friendly witnesses in a lawsuit. Another point that has come across gradually is that we do not want interviewers who are going to have their own agenda or want to exploit the occasion for their own benefit first and for the program's benefit second. I talked briefly right at the outset with Walter Cronkite one day on the telephone and he said that he had heard that someone tried to get all four past presidents together for interviews but that it did not get off the ground. After perhaps a 10- or 15-minute discussion, Cronkite said the program or project was so important that I would be remiss in my duty as Chairman if we could not proceed.

My notion of the way this would unfold is that the interviewer would go to the past president and carry on at least for an hour or so but being prepared to go back a second or third time because, inevitably, the past president will have some second thoughts, particularly after he sees a transcript of his first interview. I have told each past president that he can be involved in the editing and that none of the so-called "out takes" will be available to anyone outside the Commission. That is where we may run into problems with a producer, particularly if he is a producer of the show business variety.

We want these programs to be something that after the showing on television, copies should be placed in every college in the United States with a particular emphasis on particular research groups, political science.

I was in the room when the Chief talked with Walter Cronkite, after which we discussed him as the interviewer. The Chief liked and respected Cronkite, but he was a little fearful that since Cronkite was such a well-known celebrity the audience might focus their attention on him, the interviewer, at the expense of focusing exclusively on the president being interviewed. The interviewer was to be simply a conduit, a means by which *all* focus was directed to the president. So, after discussing a number of individuals, we landed on Hugh Sidey. Presidents Nixon, Ford and Reagan were quite pleased with Mr. Sidey; President Carter had some apprehension. But the Chief reassured President Carter that Mr. Sidey would not be permitted to show political bias or ask any unfair questions. To ensure this, the Chief drew up the questions that Mr. Sidey was to ask and when the interview actually took place, the Chief sat in the audience to ensure that all proceeded fairly. Mr. Sidey conducted all four interviews with great integrity, and there was never any question about his impartiality.

I will never forget the circumstances of the announcement to the Chief of my resignation as Staff Director. I fixed a date in my mind when I would tell him, and for a full week before that announcement, I just could not sleep. I had profound respect for the man, and it was genuinely a heartbreaking thing for me to tell him that I would be leaving. On the day of my announcement, and I can still remember exactly where I was sitting and where he was sitting, he was busy attending to some matter with his head down, when I just blurted it out that I would be leaving the Commission. I will never, never forget what happened next: His flurry of activity stopped dead, his head slowly came up and he just stared at me, saying nothing but looking, I guess the best word is, forlorn. He was not angry. He was not happy. He just stared. He tried for a while to talk me out of it by discussing activities we could work on together in the future, but he could see that I was firmly resolved to return to Hillsdale College. I remember telling him one of the major reasons for my departure: During my time at USIA and at the Bicentennial Commission, Congress constantly micromanaged or tried to micromanage everything we or I did. There was ultimately no autonomy, no independence, really no separation of powers. Congress held the purse strings and they reminded you of that daily. You did things their way or they earmarked it their way. I remember my very words, "Chief, I no longer respect Congress and I do not wish any longer to work with them." He said nothing in disagreement with my assessment.

When I resigned from the Commission, I wrote a memo to the Commissioners explaining my reasons, stating among other things that I was resigning "with a heavy heart, especially out of my fondness and respect for the Chief." I knew that as a member of the private Trust I would continue to work with the Chief, but not on a daily basis as had been the case. The Chief very kindly held a huge farewell reception for me at the Supreme Court, giving me a variety of gifts and allowing a number of family pictures with him. The gift I revere most is his bust of Benjamin Franklin, with a plaque on it that reads: "Presented to Hon. Ronald L. Trowbridge by Chief Justice Warren E. Burger January 3, 1990." The Chief originally sculpted it in 1923 at the age of 15.

On January 31, 1990, after some time for reflection, I wrote the Chief the following thank-you letter for all that he had done for me. The sentiment in it I meant then and still mean. No doubt he thought my letter "Mediterranean" (he once referred to one judge as "Mediterranean"), but so be it. I was entirely candid in the letter. Besides, he was Mediterranean too: put him in the company of children and his eyes would tear.

January 31, 1990
Honorable Warren E. Burger
2456 N. Wakefield Court
Arlington, VA

Dear Chief:

I deliberately wanted some space of time and distance between us so that I might write a more reflective thank-you note to you. Of the cocktail reception at your home, followed by the dinner at the City Tavern Club and of the farewell reception at the Supreme Court, let me simply but deeply say that I shall cherish those events forever. A photo album of the Court reception and your Franklin bust presently grace my office desk, on immediate and conspicuous view to all who enter my office. I am always eager to volunteer an explanation of them whether the entrant inquires or not.

But there are intangibles yet more important to me: your friendship; the many memoirs over the years that you enabled me to hear; and, most important in a pragmatic way, the lessons you taught me. In my position now as Vice President I do many things that I am consciously aware you instilled in me—how to manage, how to organize, how to control, how to spend, how not to spend, how to work with people, how to make hard decisions, how to attempt to be a statesman, a gentleman and a man of integrity—though on these last three I will always pale in comparison to you.

Let this note end on a continued happy refrain: the lessons will continue; I will stay in touch—and not just on Trust matters but on other matters that have a bearing on our mutual missions.

Please give my warm regards to Mrs. Burger, whom I shall miss. Pam, too, wants me to send her very best to both of you.

Sincerely,

I returned to Hillsdale College in January of 1990, and shortly thereafter asked the Chief if he would consent to give our Commencement address in May. He kindly agreed to do so, mostly, I learned, as a personal favor to me. He delivered a speech about the Soviet Union and the progress towards freedom being made there, following the recent fall in November of 1989 of the Berlin Wall. During his speech, he related the relevancy of the founding of this country and of our Constitution to the founding of the new country, as it were, in the former Soviet Union, and the problems they would have, wishing Mr. Gorbachev the best of luck in transforming the new world in Russia.

The Chief did a wonderful thing at this Commencement, which later was remarked as the highlight of the entire Commencement for students and parents. He literally stood on stage, welcomed and shook the hands of each of the 233 graduates crossing the stage to receive diplomas. No other Commencement speaker at Hillsdale College, to my knowledge, has ever done this. This took about an hour and half to do, which might seem like no large achievement, but we must remember that the Chief suffered from polio when he was a youth, and as a result suffered a three-inch curvature of the spine, which required that he wear a brace. He often needed shock therapy and was in chronic pain. When you combine this pain with the fact that when he stood on stage he was 82 years old, it was no easy task. But *he* wanted to congratulate each graduate personally; we remember again his fondness for young people, including college students. He was, among other things, Chancellor of the College of William and Mary.

In introducing the Chief for the Commencement Address, the president of Hillsdale College, George Roche, observed:

> At Hillsdale we underscore that Chief Justice Burger is a guardian of the Constitution—the limited government that it defines, the justice it

promotes, the freedom it protects, and the creativity it unleashes. He is also a statesman, scholar and historian. As a young boy, he read voraciously about the early history of this country. Out of this grew an extraordinary knowledge of history, law, justice and freedom. At the remarkable age of 15, he would sculpt a bust of Benjamin Franklin, symbolic of the direction his life would take.

Today, as Chairman of the Bicentennial Commission, he continues to give generously of his time—during the week shuffling between the Supreme Court and Commission staff offices, and over the weekends writing historical essays and books. He also continues his work on prison reform. He has visited prisons all over the world and has written on and organized conferences for the improvement of correctional facilities.

Chief Justice Burger honors Hillsdale College by allowing Hillsdale College to honor him as Chief Justice, leader in improved Court Administration, scholar, statesman, historian, painter, and sculptor—in sum, a true renaissance man in the spirit of the humanities.

Sections of his Commencement address, never printed, are worth citing; they show his humor, his affection for young people, what he believes to be the most important words in the Constitution, his assessment of Russia's difficulty in moving toward democracy, his views of President Reagan's term "evil empire," and his charge to college graduates:

> Mr. President, members of the Faculty, students, graduates of Hillsdale, and friends of Hillsdale. I think with all these other colors here today, I have an obligation to explain this scarlet robe. It did not come to me from the University of Moscow. But if Mr. Gorbachev continues his good behavior and great leadership, I am available to the University of Moscow.
>
> A good many years ago, during the summer that I was 15 years old, I was working in a boys' camp. With a family of seven children, our parents could not send us to boys' camps, but I worked in this camp. I was the truck driver and the camp bugler. I helped with the swimming teams and as a lifeguard, and in driving that truck I went around the coun-

tryside in western Wisconsin to buy corn on the cob, potatoes and all of the things that 100 boys and staff would need to keep them going . . . .

Sometimes in a group, with students particularly, I have been asked, what are the most important words in the Constitution? And I have had to think through and answer, and my answer is, if you want to hold me to one place, that the most important words embraced in the concept of the Constitution are the first three words, "We the people." That Constitution wasn't like Magna Carta where the Monarch reluctantly yielded some rights to the people—not very many rights and not to very many people, but yielded some rights which the Monarch had only kept to himself. Here it was, "We the people" who created this government.

Then I go on to respond—if you now press me, I really can't pick the most important—that surely one of the most important parts of that Constitution is embraced in eleven words in this Constitution, and it's on a relatively mundane thing: Congress shall have power, it tells us, "to regulate Commerce with foreign Nations and among the several States." Those eleven words are some of the most important in this great historic document that was the first of its kind in all history to be put to work and one that has lasted longer than any other written constitution in all history . . . .

We may as well adjust ourselves—and you should particularly because it's now in your world—that this [conversion in Russia from communism to democracy] is going to be painful, not easy, for since 1939 these Eastern European countries have had no experience with democracy. There is no institutional memory of how democracy works; they do not know what is a precinct caucus where a few neighbors gather at one neighbor's home to decide who's going to be the delegate to the county convention of a particular political party. They've got to learn that from the ground up, and in Russia itself there has never been any experience as we know. Up to 1917 there were the czars.

I might digress a moment. Sometimes as students gather, a student would ask belligerently, "Why did President Reagan call the Soviet Union the 'evil empire?'" My answer is, if someone asks me, that the Soviet Union has been an evil empire. This is going back two or three years ago—probably more evil than the empire of the Czars that existed before that. The Czars are not known to have killed millions of people in political conflict as the Communists have.

Now as for Mr. Gorbachev, if he means his stated objectives, we should be all for him. We should remember him in our prayers. We should certainly hope for his political success because his success will be ours and his failure will fall on your generation . . . . I suggest to you that you should be prepared for these remarkable changes that will affect the lives of every person in this country, every person all over the world, your children, and your grandchildren.

The torch that's being passed to you is one that may singe and burn you, but if I were to make any suggestions as to how you should handle all of these problems, it would be that these are your times, this is your world, make it a point to see that you have something to say about it.

The Chief charged no honorarium for his Commencement address, a rare and generous act indeed; most prestigious speakers demand substantial fees. Hillsdale College awarded him the degree of Doctor of Public Service.

On the matter of the "evil empire," the Chief foresaw the fall of the Berlin Wall. In remarks delivered to the German-American Constitutional Law Conference on October 24, 1989, the Chief began his speech:

The Berlin Wall is crumbling, not physically at the moment, but politically, psychologically and with enormous potential economic consequences. Just how great will be the impact on the economics of Europe remains to be seen, but that wall has been too long a symbol conflicting with the concept of the European Community and the Common Market—and the ideas of freedom. History shows that when nations built walls it was usually to keep enemies out; the Berlin Wall was to keep people in, and, from the day it was built, it was as surely doomed as Hitler's thousand-year Reich; all history teaches us that people cannot be kept in very long by walls. At one time in our earliest years our people were forbidden to migrate beyond the Appalachian Mountains—but the people ignored that barrier.

Three weeks later, the Wall came down. I asked the Chief who was primarily responsible for the fall of the Wall, and he answered, "President Reagan," and gave the reasons for it, which I jotted down. I then sent the following letter to President Reagan, citing verbatim the Chief's arguments as to why Reagan was responsible for the fall of the Wall; the Chief believed that Reagan was responsible even though Bush was serving as President at the time the Wall actually fell:

January 3, 1990

Dear President Reagan:

I wish to share with you a conversation I had yesterday with my boss, Chief Justice Burger. He stated that were the decision his, he would have selected you as *Time*'s Man of the Decade. This followed my question to him of who's responsible for all of the incredible movements away from Communism in Eastern Europe. The Chief argues that you are the individual initially and principally responsible for these events, for the following reason: your actions in Grenada, Libya, and the Persian Gulf preempted Soviet involvement in these areas. The Soviets, asserts the Chief, would surely have moved into the vacuum of the Persian Gulf had you not intervened first.

Your actions in Grenada, Libya, and the Persian Gulf joined with other "combined pressures" on the Soviet Union, resulting in the Soviet's withdrawal from Afghanistan and subsequent decisions not to intervene in Poland, then Hungary, then East Berlin . . . on down the line to Romania. In sum, actions initiated by you later joined with other pressures to bring down the Berlin Wall and to end not only the cold war but institutionalized Communism in virtually all of Eastern Europe.

President Reagan sent me the following handwritten response (Figure 6):

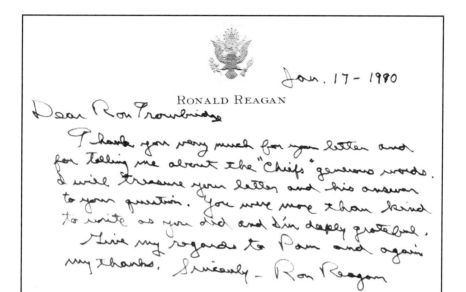

RONALD REAGAN

Jan. 17 - 1980

Dear Ron Trowbridge

Thank you very much for your letter and for telling me about the "Chiefs" generous words. I will treasure your letter and his answer to your question. You were more than kind to write as you did and I'm deeply grateful. Give my regards to Pam and again my thanks. Sincerely - Ron Reagan

Figure 6

PHOTOGRAPHS

Our moot court case at Oxford University.

The moot court team at the Middle Temple in London.
Left to right: Bob Clare, Tom O'Connor, Lord Wilberforce, the Chief,
Richard Morris, Lord Bridge, Herb Brownell and Lloyd Cutler.

The Chief before the Inaugural float he designed,
with George Washington (RLT).

*The Inaugural float. It was from this very spot that I sadly
watched President Reagan's helicopter rise above the White House,
circle the Capitol Building, and then depart for the last time.*

The float in the parade.

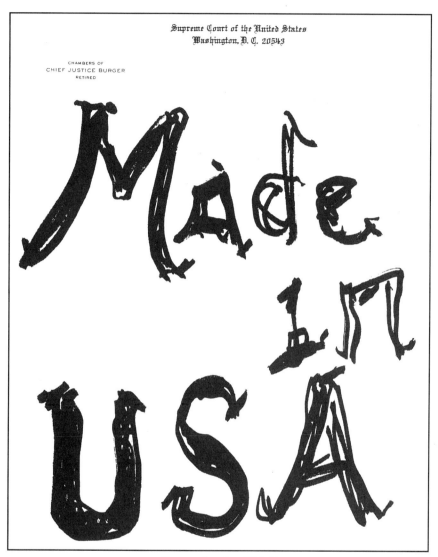

Drawn by the Chief.

PHOTO PROVIDED BY RONALD L. TROWBRIDGE

Colonial Williamsburg tailoring the replica of George Washington's suit for President Bush's Inaugural Parade.

The Chief's quick sketch of our Inaugural float.

For Pam Trowbridge
with all the best
Warren E Burger

Colonel O'Meara reports that the Chief said about this photo,
"This isn't a good photo to have around. I have a glass of wine in my
hand and am engrossed in conversation with another man's wife."

The Chief explaining the Bicentennial Commission's map contest to students. My daughter Elizabeth appears in the upper right-hand corner.

A lighter moment during our presentation in a Congressional caucus room.

The carriage carrying George Washington from Mt. Vernon to New York City.

The Chief presenting gifts at my farewell party at the Court.

PHOTO BY TODD LANCASTER

*The Franklin bust that the Chief sculpted
(at age 15) and inscribed to me.*

PHOTO PROVIDED COURTESY OF THE BICENTENNIAL COMMISSION

*My family at the farewell party at the Court.
Andrew, Stephen, Pamela, and Elizabeth.*

*My farewell party. Left to right: Lloyd Culter,
the Chief, RLT and Burnett Anderson.*

*The Chief receiving an honorary doctorate
from President George Roche at
Hillsdale College's Commencement.*

With his law clerk Ken Starr, 1976-1977.

PHOTO PROVIDED BY THE HONORABLE KEN STARR

With Burnett Anderson years ago.

PHOTO PROVIDED BY BURNETT ANDERSON

Mrs. Burger in the Anderson kitchen.

The wine rack the Chief made for Burnett and Pia Anderson.

PHOTO BY TODD LANCASTER

The Chief's painting of the Chief Justice
on the wine rack.

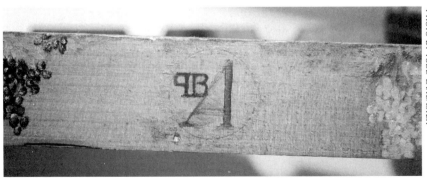

PHOTO BY TODD LANCASTER

Initials for Pia and Burnett Anderson.

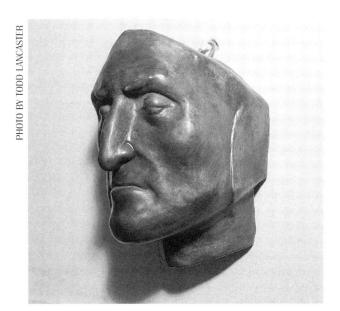

PHOTO BY TODD LANCASTER

The Dante death mask that the Chief sculpted.

FRANZ JANIZEN,
COLLECTION OF THE SUPREME COURT OF THE UNITED STATES

*The bas-relief of Chief Justice John Marshall
that the Chief sculpted. It now hangs
in the Chief Justice's dining room at the Court.*

PHOTO BY TODD LANCASTER

PHOTO BY TODD LANCASTER

*The Chief's wine coaster, with the quarter in the
center featuring George Washington.*

The pallbearers with the Chief's casket, approaching the Supreme Court.
Note the lone spectator on the left,
holding the umbrella portraying the American flag.

The pallbearers approaching the Court. Members of the
Supreme Court are lined up on the steps on the right.

PHOTO BY RONALD L. TROWBRIDGE

The Chief's bier in the Supreme Court. Standing on guard to the right
is Judge Michael Luttig, a former law clerk and close friend of the Chief.

PHOTO BY RONALD L. TROWBRIDGE

The memorial tribute at The National Presbyterian Church.
Justices Anthony Kennedy and Clarence Thomas are standing on the left.

PHOTO BY RONALD L. TROWBRIDGE

*Justice Sandra Day O'Connor about to hug the Chief's son, Wade.
Justice O'Connor had just placed a flower on the Chief's casket.*

Chapter 10

Interview with Burnett Anderson

Burnett Anderson's government service included: Press Officer for the Marshall Plan agencies in Germany, 1952-54; Director of Press Relations, U.S. Information Agency, Washington, 1954; Deputy Director of Press and Publications Service, USIA, responsible for worldwide news and publications and two overseas printing plants, 1955-57; Counselor for Public Affairs, U.S. Embassy, Iran, 1957-60; National War College, 1960-61; appointment as Associate Deputy Director of USIA (Policy) by Director Edward R. Murrow, 1961; Deputy Director (Policy) under Directors Carl Rowan and Leonard Marks, 1964-67; Counselor for Public Affairs, U.S. Embassy Madrid, 1967-69; Paris, 1969-77; London, 1977-79. Presidential appointment as Career Minister in 1971.

His private employment included: Press Secretary and speech writer to Governors Harold E. Stassen and Edward J. Thye of Minnesota, 1941-44; newspaper reporter, political writer, and foreign correspondent 1944-52 (for Minneapolis *Star and Tribune*, *LOOK* Magazine, and ABC-Radio).

Among his awards and publications were: Edward R. Murrow Award for Excellence in Public Diplomacy, Tufts University, 1972; Hutchison Medal of the University of Rochester for Distinguished Public Service, 1977; USIA Distinguished Service Award, 1963; Arthur S. Fleming Award to Outstanding Young Men in the Federal Service, 1956; co-author of *EQUAL JUSTICE, The Supreme Court in American Life*; editor of *Delivery of Justice*, the public papers of Chief Justice Warren E. Burger; consulting editor, *The Illustrated History of the Supreme Court*; editor of or contributor to other books on the Supreme Court.

RT: I think, from all that I know about you and in discussing you with the Chief, that you were —without question—his very best friend. And there is no person who is in close second place. Do you have any reason to suggest that that's not accurate?

BA: No, I think it's very accurate. I don't know of anybody outside his family—outside his wife, probably—that spent as much time with him over the last dozen years, last two decades as I did. We were together on long walks. We spent a lot of time in his office, and during the early '80s when I was doing a lot of writing about the Court, we spent innumerable hours together: a mix of perhaps business and friendship conversation. He was an articulate interlocutor and his memory was absolutely unbelievable. It was like a computer. He recalled names, dates, places that had long since escaped me. It was, I'm sure, a rare week that I didn't have at least something from him scribbled at his desk and sent on by his secretary, or with a little dictated note.

RT: When did you first meet him?

BA: We met in the fall of the year 1941, when I became Press Secretary to Harold Stassen, and Burger played a very interesting role in that context. He was a member of the Kitchen Cabinet, but never very visible to the public, and never sought public office himself. I know that he was offered various things, including an appointment to fill an unexpired Senate term, but he steadfastly refused to engage in that type of political activity. He didn't want a public office.

RT: The Chief seemed willing to renounce personal wealth in the interest of public service. Am I wrong in that assessment?

BA: No, you're absolutely right in that assessment. He spoke now and again to me without using figures of the amount of money he didn't make by being in public service. But let me go back a little bit to your first question.

      I met him, as I say, when I went to work for Harold Stassen, and he had been very active in the Stassen movement: the liberalization of the Minnesota Republican Party, if you will, which brought Stassen into office in the 1938 election. He [the Chief] was young himself; the whole team was young. But one of the reasons that I was taken with him was because he was so interested in young people. I don't know how much his billable hours cost at that time, but I would go around to see him to talk over something or another, and we'd sit for an hour with me just soaking up his wisdom. So that interest in young people never failed, and you know that from your own experience in the Commission that he was always aiming at the upcoming generation.

RT: Yes, he said, as a matter of fact, he was going to focus on young people, and he said, "Once you've gotten over 50, it's too late."

BA: (laughing) Well, I think that's right.

RT: He loved to be with young kids, little kids. I mean, kids in the fifth grade and kindergarten and first grade, and every time he was with them tears would come to his eyes. And so you had this perception that he's this austere, stern, sober, serious guy, but really he was just one of us, and really enjoyed being with kids.

BA: Well, you saw tears. I saw him lose control only once in these 54 years of close friendship and association. He was an extraordinarily controlled man, and I hear that he sometimes had a temper. But you know, all the time I spent with him I never saw that. He could complain pretty effectively, but I never saw him lose his temper. But only once did he break down completely, and I think this is probably worth reporting.

Five years before the anniversary of the Constitution Bicentennial (which would make it 1982), he got together a group at Williamsburg including jurists, the then Congressional Librarian, and others to talk about how to observe the Bicentennial of the Constitution, as far as the judiciary was concerned at least. And there was a Friday night working dinner that fell on Constitution day, which was also Burger's 75th birthday. He wanted me to go to the meeting, and when I realized this [the birthday] three or four days before the event, I called up his aide to ask what the plans were for his birthday, and he said, "Shhhh." Everybody was under very strict orders not to mention it, not to tell anybody about it, and above all not to do anything about it.

Well, I wasn't hired by him, so I decided what I would do about it, and I called up the Inn down there and made arrangements for the birthday cake, and when it came in with candles with the coffee, he looked very surprised. I made a brief toast saying pretty much what I thought about Warren Burger and Burger as Chief Justice of the United States. When I sat down, he was crying. He tried to control it, but he couldn't. For the next two or three minutes, Vera stepped in and kept the conversation going. That's the only time in over 50 years that I ever saw him lose complete control. [Burnett's toast follows:]

TOAST TO THE FIFTEENTH CHIEF JUSTICE OF THE UNITED STATES, WARREN BURGER, AT AN INFORMAL WORKING DINNER AT WILLIAMSBURG LODGE, WILLIAMSBURG, VIRGINIA, SEPTEMBER 17, 1982, GIVEN BY BURNETT ANDERSON

Mr. Chief Justice:

There is one important matter which is not on the agenda which I believe this group would be remiss in not addressing. The subject before us for this weekend meeting is the celebration of an anniversary, perhaps the most important in the history of representative government.

It is not without a hint of trepidation that I invite your attention to another anniversary, but I invoke one measure of absolute seniority in even this distinguished gathering. I wear the chevrons of a friendship that has prospered and deepened and withstood—for more than 40 years—the erosive action of time, profound and frequent changes in place and station, and the distance of oceans. With this ever-strengthened armor I shall, for a few moments, venture the patience of all of you and the wrath of one of you.

What I have to say may be obvious, certainly to many of you in this room, but sometimes the obvious must be said.

The Constitution of the United States is inseparable from the lives and character of those who created it and those who have made it endure. We have been fortunate beyond the laws of chance in the men who have been its principal guardians through 195 years. Today more than ever the Constitution is central to the preservation of our diverse and fragile human society. Today more than ever we are fortunate in the life and character of our Chief Justice, and today is his birthday.

This anniversary is coincidental with and incidental to the purpose of our weekend meeting, but it lends itself ideally to marking a birthday of the Fifteenth Chief Justice. He himself has characteristically issued a permanent injunction against all forms of celebration to those of his immediate circle who might be suspected of conspiracy to note the day. His writ runs far and it runs wide, but on this matter of conscience I have elected the course of civil disobedience and I am prepared to accept the lawful penalty.

This very gathering says much about Warren Burger. I find it hard—
I find it impossible—to think of another among those few persons of his
eminence in public life, national and international, whose natal anniversary would be allowed to pass without fanfare.

He, instead, is at work. The work of this weekend is also characteristic. Like much of what he does, it is above and beyond the already
awesome list of statutory duties which fill his 12- or 14-hour days and 7-
day weeks. He is, while drawing on the experience and wisdom of the
past, seizing the present to improve the future, using today to improve
tomorrow. The focus of this weekend is, after all, on an event whose
climax is still five years away.

It would be presumptuous for a layman to say anything in this distinguished company of Warren Burger the Chief Justice, the jurist, the ad-
ministrator of our judiciary, the once advocate and once assistant attorney
general, which is not to say I do not have views. But I yield to no one in
my appreciation of Warren Burger the man, and the friend.

Aesop said it first, Publilius Syrus made it a maxim, Cervantes and
Shakespeare plagiarized it: Familiarity breeds contempt. Mark Twain
put it in the American vernacular: No man is a hero to his valet.

The Fifteenth Chief Justice has over-ruled those maxims. With him,
familiarity breeds respect.

In the current popular competition to debase the language, the word
"virtue" seems almost to have disappeared. From the perspective of four
decades of association, I borrow exactly that word in a phrase from
Rousseau to illuminate the character of Chief Justice Burger: rich above
all in "the most precious thing possessed by man, the morality of his
action and the love of virtue."

Each of us here sees the Fifteenth Chief Justice through his own professional and personal windows. He touches a multitude of lives in a
multitude of ways. I will share some of my personal glimpses on this
most personal occasion.

I see him arriving at the Court on a Saturday morning after an early
hour or two in the garden, distributing sacks of vine-ripened tomatoes or
fresh spring onions to clerks and colleagues and messengers. Being caught

unawares in the back room with his sculpting tools—behind which lingers an imagined recollection of the teen-aged schoolboy with his wagon digging modeling clay from the banks of the Mississippi. Watching him in the kitchen at home or at the Court, complete with chef's apron, making a gourmet lunch for a chosen friend or two, thoughtfully remembering their favorite dishes. Escaping to the Jeu de Paume at the Louvre for an hour or so from an official schedule in Paris, letting a companion see Monet and Manet, Sisley and Pissaro as if anew through his eyes. Talking with a convict in a prison in Sweden in his never-ending search for a better penal system. Doing his own drip-dry laundry in the bathroom on travels abroad, to the astonishment of some rather highly-placed officials and their wives whose houseguest he has been.

Still full of talk after midnight on the screened porch at home, adducing Montaigne and Locke as well as Franklin and Marshall to show how Enlightenment became Law. Arriving unannounced at friends' doors at Christmas with the annual remembrance of holly branches cut with his own pruning shears. Walking, walking, walking the hills of Arlington or the streets of Washington of a Sunday afternoon, unencumbered by the apparatus of security as freely as the most anonymous citizen of the Republic. Searching the stalls of Eastern Market early of a spring Saturday morning to find the right seedlings for the weekend planting. Spending Saturday afternoon in chambers, reworking for the fifth time the draft of an opinion or major address with a sure and practiced editorial hand, striking the adjective, searching for still greater simplicity, clarity, precision.

Sitting motionless for a portrait artist, deep in thought and with a look of serene benignity. Addressing his chauffeur as considerately as he speaks with kings. And he speaks with many potentates. Exercising always the restlessly inquiring intellect: watching, listening, searching, reading, registering, processing, sifting, weighing, qualifying, comparing, nuancing, concluding, seeking the wisdom of each new day. But ever engaged with his wife and family, ever more mindful of his friends than of himself.

Mr. Chief Justice, you may serve your warrant for this intrusion into your private life at your pleasure, but not until after the company has drunk a toast. Friends, on his birthday, 1982, the Fifteenth Chief Justice of the United States.

RT: The Chief was a great man who was one of us with class. He had an ability to be with us, to work with anybody and everybody, and work at our level, and yet still maintain a statesmanship quality that made us aspire to it. You can't say he was just folks or one of the boys, but he could be with you, and he could be comfortable with you, and you wanted to be like him. You wanted to emulate that quality. He was with you and at the same time he was above you.

BA: It's just sort of the reverse of what they said about Wilkie when he stole the 1940 Presidential nomination. They called him the barefoot boy from Wall Street, and this is sort of the reverse of that.

RT: One of the things that always amazed me was the attention he paid to details. He read every word, every letter, every comma.

BA: Oh, and he was a hell of a good editor too!

RT: You better believe that everything that came out of that Court was seen; every word that came out of there was his.

BA: Oh, absolutely. I mention that in my tribute at William and Mary that when Burger made a speech you knew who was talking, and it was Burger.

RT: And, as a matter of fact, there are letters over my signature that were entirely his, and so I can say with great pride that Ron Trowbridge has been ghosted by the Chief Justice.

BA: That's an honor we share. The thing I wanted to say was that his writing and editing had one aspect that I did not like. I was never able to cure him of it. His mind worked so rapidly and was so full of whatever the matter was at hand that he'd get three sentences into editing something and start writing an insert. I'd say, "Goddamn it, Warren, that's in the next paragraph. You ought to at least glance through this before you start putting in what's already there." But he worked so rapidly that I could never stop it. It just kept on happening, and I'd have to put the brakes on and say, "Wait a minute, look a little further."

RT: You and I both know that the Chief had some flaws.

BA: I'll give you another line free that might apply in a way here, and it's in something that I wrote about him somewhere. Humility was not anywhere near the top of his list of virtues; but on the other hand, he had very little to be humble about (laughing). How do you like that?

RT: I want to talk about the notion of ethics with the Chief. I know that he could not stand lawyers who advertised. I know he favored the British system in terms of contingency fees. I know that he was almost apoplectic about prosecutors and defenders who carried on their cases before the public. I mean, if we look at the business that's going on today with the Monica Lewinsky case, attorneys are taking their case against Starr to the media. Starr doesn't have the advantage of a response, and he's staying out of the media, the way the Chief would have wished, though Starr did do that one backgrounder to Steve Brill, and I suspect the Chief might have criticized him for that.

BA: I think he would have. He was, as you say, virtually apoplectic about that sort of thing. That's a very good word. And for the last year of his life, maybe two years, he was considering resigning from the American Bar Association in protest to their refusal or inability to act on these matters. We talked about that at least a dozen times, and I sort of encouraged him because I thought it would have been a great gesture.

RT: You mean in terms of using the media in order to argue cases, contingency fees, ethics, using advertising? These things come quickly to mind, but can you think of anything else right off the top of your head?

BA: Possibly the failure to enforce stability in the court room. That business of lawyers standing in the court room and calling each other names was also an abomination.

RT: To him?

BA: Yes.

RT: You explained to me once that, right after he was selected as Chief Justice of the United States by Nixon, he retreated to your house. He came over here, I guess, to escape what—the press, or to escape notice?

BA: Well, it was really coincidental. He loved to visit, he and Vera both, and one of the reasons that our friendship flourished the way it did was that my wife Pia and Vera got along so well. They were equally good friends, and indeed, in the last dozen years or more of her life, since our return to Washington from the Foreign Service out of London in 1979, Vera's daily telephone call at 4:00 to Pia was as regular as the sunrise and sunset. That, of course, facilitated our friendship because the four of us were all perfectly in harmony. Not that it inhibited anybody stating his opinion; in fact, it encouraged it, because we knew we could trust each other so well.

They came to visit us several times overseas, and we looked forward to it as a summer event in the latter three or four years. They had planned to come and spend a little time with us in Paris the year of the Nixon [tapes] case. I spent a week doing virtually nothing except discussing the Nixon case. You see, his mind was still so full of it that whenever we had an odd, quiet moment sitting in the library in my apartment, we would get back to it.

RT: You mean the Nixon case, the release of the tapes?

BA: The Nixon case, yes, and his opinion. As you know, I deliberately did not take notes or keep any records of our conversations over the years and so I can't reconstruct it—wouldn't even try to reconstruct what he said during that week. He did say one thing that I do recall that I do think is pertinent, which is probably why I recall it: There have been all kinds of allegations about who wrote that opinion and so on, trying to detract from Burger's role in it. I think, probably, there's something in that book *The Brethren* by Woodward and Bernstein. Well, one of the things he said as we looked at the opinion (he would often pull it out and read a paragraph or point to a certain part of the opinion) was that one of the reasons this opinion is so strong and categorical, if you will, is because in drafting it, "I had to allow myself some room for negotiation." When the Associate Justices sat down over it, he said, they left in a lot more that "I was ready to take out if I had to, to get a unanimous opinion." He said he really wanted a unanimous decision on this, and that's why, among other things, it is such a clear and categorical opinion. It would certainly suggest that at least as he recalled what happened in the week or two

immediately following the great event, that it was—like everything else he put his hand to—his own opinion.

RT: And what was asserted in *The Brethren*? Were the authors advo-
cating something to the contrary?

BA: I'm not sure if it was in that book, but at the time there were
allegations that somebody else had drafted it, or at least parts of
it. There is a passage in my tribute at William and Mary about
everything being the Chief's own. "When Warren Burger made
a public speech you knew who was talking. He never employed
a speech writer. His occasional articles for publication were also
entirely his own work. He respected his audiences, and never
cheated them. He gave them only of himself."

RT: He was a product of the Depression; what kind of mark do you
think that left on him?

BA: We talked about it a great deal. I was quite equally a child of the
Depression. He was somewhat older and was married at that
time, and every once in a while he would run across a piece of
paper or something that reminded him of it. In fact, he showed
me some receipts from about 1934 that had been carefully preserved and had recently turned up. Of course, the figures were
absolutely ridiculous: renting a house for, say, $25 a month or
something like that, which you could do in those days.

RT: What was your feeling about the philosophy or the political nature of the man?

BA: Well, that's a big subject that really made much of his career
ironical. But he was actively opposed to the conservative wing

of the Republican Party from the beginning. In the early 1940s, when I was Harold Stassen's Press Secretary, I engaged in a little politicking and had Burger's assistance in some rather—what should I say—I won't say dirty politics, but something like that, in mounting attacks on what we called the old guard. And that was as active a fight in Minnesota in the 1940s as it is today in the entire nation. He was definitely, very much one of the progressive or moderate Republicans, as they referred to themselves at that time. My brother-in-law, Bernard LeVander, was also part of that movement. As a very idealistic, highly liberal, socially-minded young man, he was very comfortable with Stassen and Burger, who shared these views and tried to carry them out, tried to apply them. He has now quit the Republican Party of Minnesota because of the extent to which it has cow-towed to the arch-conservatives. So I would put Burger—well, let me put it this way: In their latter years, I would put Burger on your scale of one to ten at, probably, five or six; Hubert Humphrey, on the other end, was a three or four. They were that close. And, of course, they were great personal friends.

So, the belief at the time when Nixon chose him was that he was a conservative, and that belief let him waltz through Congress with nary a negative voting voice, which was very, very ironical to me. I'm an Independent.

RT: I often thought his temperament was quite traditional, and I didn't see him as anything of a radical person in that sense.

BA: No, but he was not at all opposed to the government stepping in where it was necessary. That comes through in many different ways. He saw the need for legislation in the changing society, the differences between this society and when the Constitution was written.

RT: He was obviously a deep man. You don't want to oversimplify the whole person.

BA: No, you can't. You see, he was a very complicated man, too. I think it should be added that this line of reasoning about the Constitution was stimulated in part by the Bicentennial celebration of '76 when there was a lot of speaking on the subject of the 200 years since the Declaration of Independence. He spoke about this in the context of how dramatically successful this country had been as compared with those that are under some kind of authoritarian rule. I don't think it went to the question of whether the government should or should not intervene in any given situation as it might be required. Rather, the freedom to develop your talents and apply them without any authoritarian stricture was the explanation for the success of the American experiment.

RT: One of the speeches he made a point of sending to me was one he made before Georgy Arbatov in Moscow, and that's exactly his point: looking at our society, talking about the history of how ours evolved, and talking about the unleashed freedoms that people can have as a result of the Constitution—comparing all this to the different situation in Russia under Communism.

BA: I want to go back on one point, so it doesn't get lost, on public service. Are you familiar with the public service that he did in St. Paul? Long before he tied up with Stassen he was extremely active in city politics. St. Paul at that time (and I know this part because I lived about 75 miles from there) was a haven for gangsters. Utterly corrupt. When things got too hot in Chicago, the gangsters would come up and cool off in St. Paul. There was a pact, if you will, unwritten, perhaps it just developed gradually, that the mobs would leave St. Paul alone as long as St. Paul left them alone. So St. Paul was a cooling off place for the mobs in the 1930s. Burger was highly influential in changing the law, reforming the police, driving the gangsters out of St. Paul and making it a very clean town. He served in various other contexts at that time. In 1936, he was President of the Junior Chamber of Commerce, and he made a speech on the growing national debt and the dangers thereof when the national debt was probably not even a billion dollars.

RT: Was he ever threatened when he tried to get rid of the gangsters in St. Paul?

BA: Probably not. I think that if they were going to kill people, they'd have had to shoot a lot of them. But the situation in St. Paul was such that I, for one, would have thought twice before engaging visibly in any effort to change things.

RT: So at least potentially he was running the risk of his own life.

BA: That history is on record a little bit somewhere, and it shows that his words about public service, even as a very young man, were not just empty rhetoric. He applied them.

RT: The Chief once told me that as a youngster with polio he had been confined to bed for a long period of time during which he read about the history of the country.

BA: Yes, that is right. He was fascinated by history. I can't think that the disease had any essential effect on his career beyond the acquisition of a little bit more knowledge than he would have otherwise had at that point.

He talked about his polio very, very matter-of-factly, just as you'd talk about the weather. It was just like anything else, you had to live with it. You couldn't do anything about it.

I'll give you something that might be useful. He had this terrible hit-and-run accident. He was walking or bicycling and somebody hit him. It left its mark, including a lame foot—I don't know the nature of the injury, but I know it made it difficult for him to wear shoes. He was visiting us in Paris, and the Ambassador was having a formal dinner party for him. We were dressing and he came out wearing Swedish wooden shoes. He said they were the only thing that was really comfortable. Vera said, "Warren, you can't go to the Ambassadorial residence dinner in wooden shoes." He said, "Well, stand by and you'll see it happen." Not only did he do that, but he wore them with his tux to a dinner given by the mayor of Paris—now President Chirac. And there we sat after dinner, yacking away and Warren sitting cross-legged with wooden shoes swinging in the breeze.

RT: I never saw him in anything other than what looked like Hush Puppies. I knew the reason for that, of course, was his back. And now you say his foot, too.

BA: He wore those Australian shoes that were somewhat like Hush Puppies; those were his real favorites. I can't remember the brand name, but they were a very comfortable suede shoe.

RT: Burnett, tell the story about the Chief being a gourmet cook and what your wife said to him one day.

BA: This was during the post-Nixon-opinion visit, and, of course, the word "opinion" was being bandied about constantly. Burger came out in the kitchen one day where Vera was sitting with Pia, while she was cooking red cabbage. He came over and took the cover off, saying, "Oh, I see you're cooking red cabbage. Did you do [so and so]?" Then he launched into a set of instructions as how best to cook red cabbage. Finally Pia turned to Vera and said, "Vera, would you please tell that man of yours that nobody in this kitchen asked for his opinion." It brought a good laugh, particularly from Warren.

It was an earlier visit, I think, when he followed up on a Christmas present. There was a season when he was very much in the business of making wine racks. He came here for Christmas dinner, as he did two or three times when Vera was away, and again after Vera's death—we make a lot of Christmas in our household as he did in his. So that year he came and gave us a wine rack. This was while I was in Washington on one of my assignments here. Later he caught up with us in Paris where we were using the rack, and looked at it and said, "Oh, I forgot to finish painting this, and I didn't sign it." So I got out my paints, and he set up shop in our little pantry, which was a very light and pleasant room between our kitchen and big dining room in the Paris apartment. I got out, at his request, a beret like the traditional French artist is supposed to have worn, and got him a little glass of Scotch whiskey, which he hid behind the door with some Swedish hors d'oeuvres that we had prepared for him. He sat and finished putting the decorative elements on the wine rack and finished it off with a little vignette of a retreating Justice with a black robe and white hair. [See photo, page 98.] Of course, this is something that we treasure very, very greatly and that was also a typical Burger gesture. And let me make one point here that you'll want to follow up. Burger had very good friends, and one of the reasons was he worked hard at keeping them.

RT: I have here, Burnett, your comments to the College of William and Mary on Friday, April 12, 1996. What was the occasion?

BA: That was the formal acceptance of Burger's papers and other memorabilia by William and Mary [after his death], with Margaret Thatcher making the formal acceptance. Burger had been Chancellor for several years, and Thatcher succeeded him. She was kind enough to come around for a large luncheon at the college and make the formal acceptance. A couple of weeks before it was on, the President of the college called me and said that they had everything that they needed for the occasion except someone who could speak about Burger himself. In view of my long friendship, would I do that? And, of course, I said that I would be delighted to tell the world how I feel about Warren Burger the human being. The result was a brief and rather successful speech. I hesitate to say this for fear of being accused of self promotion. Mrs. Thatcher, of course, got very, very handsome applause, and when I finished my speech on Burger, I had to return twice to the dais (for the first and only time in my life) to acknowledge the continuing loud applause. It was an occasion that turned out to be very moving for me as well. [Burnett's tribute follows:]

REMARKS
THE COLLEGE OF WILLIAM AND MARY IN VIRGINIA
FRIDAY, APRIL 12, 1996

Madame Chancellor, Mr. President, Distinguished Faculty and Guests:

Curiously, but not illogically, this is the second time in 14 years that I have risen here in Williamsburg to speak of my great friend Warren Burger. The first time I was speaking to him. The date was September 17, 1982, a Friday. The locus was Williamsburg Lodge; the occasion, an informal working dinner. The timing and nature of the gathering alone say a good deal about our Fifteenth Chief Justice.

Some two dozen prominent jurists and other leaders from across the country had been brought together by the Chief to make plans for the celebration of the Bicentennial of the Constitution in 1987. One could say it was a typical Burger business meeting. It was held on a weekend, it continued over all meals, and it dealt with a matter still five years ahead. To the day. Earlier in the week, it had occurred to me that the Friday date was not only the 195th anniversary of the Constitution, it was to be the 75th birthday of Warren Burger. I got in touch with the Chief's secretary to find out what the plans were for observing the big anniversary. She almost whispered in replying that the Chief had issued the firmest, most categorical instructions that there was to be not even a mention of the birthday anniversary, on the pain of contempt, if not execution.

Conniving with the kitchen staff of the Lodge, I arranged for a candle-lit birthday cake to be brought in over coffee at the Friday dinner.

A surprised Chief Justice looked up as I rose to say that I could think of no other public person of his national and international eminence whose 75th anniversary would be allowed to pass without celebration. Instead of celebration, Warren Burger was at work, and work characteristic of him. It was labor above and beyond the awesome list of some 35 statutory duties that filled his 12-hour days and 7-day work weeks. Typically, he was drawing on the wisdom of the past, and exploiting the present to improve the future, using today to reach for a better tomorrow. The papers and memorabilia now in the trusted care of William and Mary College will give historians a full account of a remarkable Chief Justice of the United States.

No history of the Constitution of the United States, no full understanding of it, would be complete without even only two of his landmark decisions, to say nothing of the full body of 17 years of interpretation. No record of the American judiciary would be complete without his contribution: in the opinion of many of his most knowledgeable peers, Warren Burger did more than any single person in history to improve the operation of all our nation's courts.

But my principal concern today is the record of the whole man, the oversize dimensions of a figure which will only grow with the passage of time. I had the good fortune to share personally in more than 50 of Chief Justice Burger's four-score and seven active years. Many among you have a profound understanding of his professional career and accomplishments, but I yield to no one in my knowledge and appreciation of Burger the Man.

The Constitution, like all human institutions, is inseparable from the lives and the character of those who created it, and those who have made it endure. In the life and character of our fifteenth Chief Justice, we were particularly fortunate. Rising from modest beginnings in the midwest, he developed a moral and ethical compass that pointed unerringly to the true pole of virtue. His character was impeccable; his civility, unfailing and unmatched.

Warren Burger's range of interests and talents was as fulsome as the energies he brought to expressing them. He was a good deal more than a duffer as a sculptor. Indeed, some of you may have a specimen of one of his earliest efforts. As a means of raising funds for the Constitution Bicentennial educational activities, the Franklin Mint persuaded Burger to authorize reproduction and sale of a small bust of Benjamin Franklin. It was done in Burger's teens, molded of clay dug up from the banks of the nearby Mississippi River, and hauled home by the young artist in his wagon.

His interest in sculpture and painting never lessened. It was a great experience to wander the Jeu de Paume at the Louvre with him and see Monet and Manet, Sisley and Pisarro as if anew through his eyes. And you can examine his late sculptural efforts at the Supreme Court if you know where to look. They were never publicized.

Warren Burger had green thumbs on both hands, and as long as he was able he used them to the limit. He loved gardening, and trees, and shrubs. I can visualize him now, arriving at the Court on a Saturday morning, distributing vine-ripened tomatoes or fresh spring onions to colleagues and clerks and messengers. Or you might find him at a different stage of the food chain, in the kitchen at home or his small kitchen at the Court, complete with chef's apron, making a gourmet lunch for a chosen friend or two, thoughtfully remembering their favorite dishes.

We who were fortunate enough to have had Warren Burger as a friend all have our own panoply of recollections. I see him still in a hundred guises. On the screened porch at home, still full of talk after midnight, adducing Montaigne and Locke as well as Jefferson and Marshall to show how Enlightenment became Law. Arriving at the door of a friend at Christmas with the annual remembrance of holly branches cut from his own tree beside the old house in Arlington. Donning the ribbon and medallion to attend a meeting of the Tastevin society; he was proud of his knowledge of wines and his cellar. Squatting on the sidewalk at the Eastern Market early of a spring Saturday morning to find the right seedlings for weekend planting. Walking, walking, walking the hills of Arlington or the streets of Capitol Hill of a Sunday afternoon, unencumbered by the apparatus of security, as freely as the most anonymous citizen of the Republic. In the most secluded rooms of chambers, reworking the draft of an opinion or a major address with a sure editorial hand, striking the adjective, searching for clarity, simplicity, precision.

When Warren Burger made a public speech, you knew who was talking. He never employed a speech writer. His occasional articles for publication were also entirely his own work. He respected his audiences, never cheated them. He gave them only of himself.

He was, above all, true to his family and his origins. He was ever thoughtful of his wife, his son and daughter, and more mindful of his friends than of himself. The folk wisdom of his family would often pop up unexpectedly. Discussing the speed and energy with which he went to work on the overburdened judicial system immediately after confirmation as Chief Justice, Burger commented: "My grandmother used to say that when you moved in to a new house, you should fix the cracks in the plaster right away, before you get used to them."

Chief Justice Rehnquist made a telling observation in a moving eulogy. He speculated that in his new location Warren Burger was already laying out some plans for improvements to St. Peter.

Warren Burger's life had meaning for all of us. He has moved on into the stream of history, the content and course of which he himself helped greatly to shape. We have been enriched by his presence among us. Let us count it our good fortune that this great institution will preserve the record and share those riches with generations still to come.

RT: When the Chief died, I attended the ceremony here in Washington at the church, and then, of course, the funeral at Arlington Cemetery. I saw that you were very closely involved with the family and were attendant with them and obviously one of those deeply involved in the whole process. Chief Justice Rehnquist, Justice O'Connor, and Judge Luttig spoke, and I thought you might have spoken. Why didn't you?

BA: There were two reasons. One, this was a formal occasion at which the judicial side was being emphasized, but, more important, because I wasn't sure I could control myself. His loss has left an absolutely major hole that is as keen today as it was the day he died, and I have trouble speaking about him even with you without very deep emotion.

RT: Did he resign [as Chief Justice] because he wanted to commemorate the Bicentennial appropriately?

BA: The short answer is yes. The qualified answer is that after you've been doing one thing—even the fascinating kind of thing that he was doing—for 17 years, it starts getting to be pretty repetitive. And in weighing his options, I'm sure that he felt that most of his attainable goals had been achieved during that period. Second,

I'm sure that he was aware of his place in history. He had achieved a length of stay that was the longest of any Chief Justice in this century and, with only 14 years left [in the century], could not be exceeded in this century. I think *that*, perhaps, figured in a very small way in the timing of the decision. But, also, again, coming to young people. He felt as he had for so long that the Constitution was simply not well enough known and understood and that if he could somehow succeed in getting it more widely known and understood and applied by the upcoming generation, that was as worthy a work as a man could undertake.

RT: He made a curious comment to me once. We were talking about the business of racial set asides and Affirmative Action, and he said that he endorsed special treatment of blacks, not Hispanics, not native Americans, not women, not Muslims, not anybody else but blacks. He said the reason for that was that they did not come to this country on their own accord, that they were brought here as slaves, and that therefore we had a moral obligation to give them special treatment.

BA: He made exactly the same point with me. In many discussions involving the racial problems of one kind or another, he said we brought them here probably against their will, and we owe them something.

RT: I once asked him what he thought about flag burning. Since this Court decision had already been made and he therefore felt he could comment on it, he defined it not as expression or speech, but as "conduct," and cited Hugo Black and a similar flag-burning precedent. As you know, Justice Scalia and others have defined flag burning as a form of expression.

BA: I don't remember anything specific on flag burning, but he did in other contexts make the distinction between expression and conduct, and I think probably he would have gone that way. I think he would have tried to find a way to justify it with precedent.

Let me say something on my own here in regard to him and opinions. He was extraordinarily discreet, even with me, in regard to the business of the Court. As various major opinions came along, we would discuss them, sometimes at length, and I would ask him about them. I learned a great deal about the Constitution from him in these conversations. I would ask him about the case, and he would present to me the issues involved and the arguments on both sides. Now, over a period of 15 years we had this kind of constant discussion of what was going on in the Court. He discussed even major cases, "on the one hand and on the other hand." Only once (this is how good he was in terms of articulating and keeping his opinion to himself) did I predict with confidence how he was going to rule. Three weeks before the decision came down that overruled a congressional veto (one house veto) of legislation, I came home and told my wife, I know how he's going to go on this one. But that was the first time, and that was after at least a dozen years of constant discussion of various cases that were coming up before the Supreme Court.

RT: He'd obviously listen to all sides of the argument without preconceived notions. He once told me that he personally, emotionally did not favor the death penalty, but said because it's in the Constitution, he would therefore comply with it.

BA: Oh, yes. That was our understanding whenever we talked about it. We were both emotionally opposed to it, or personally opposed to it. But with the qualification that the substitute of life sentence had to be a true life sentence and not subject to parole.

RT: I have his working draft of a piece on gun control; he was working this thing out in his mind, and he sent it down to me.

BA: Sometimes it'd take years before something jelled.

RT: Or he'd send down the first version, then I'd get the second draft, then the third, and I could see he was honing it, tightening it and deleting certain things.

BA: On that book of his speeches I compiled, I think I'd got seven or eight drafts done over a period of two or three years before we finally agreed on everything and it went to press. But on gun control, you know, that was night and day for him. It was obvious if you could license anything, you could in effect license guns in the same way that you license cars and other things that are not forbidden by the Constitution.

You mentioned his sense of humor, and of course he had a great one. But it did not extend to repeating so-called jokes of the week or jokes of the day. I can't recall his ever passing on the kind of joke that moves around. His sense of humor was his own. And his wit was his own.

RT: I think people might find it surprising, but he used to tease me.

BA: Oh, he teased the life out of his friends, and his kids.

RT: He'd tease me, and I'd tease him back. And then he'd hold his index finger up like a gun and pull the trigger.

BA: That shows not only how fond he was of you, but how much he trusted you, because he would tease the life out of Vera. Sometimes you'd think, if you didn't know them, or if you were standing on a nearby corner hearing them, you'd think they were really having a scrap, but it was really him teasing her. And she didn't take anything from him at all.

RT: He didn't seem to carry much money; I guess he just didn't care much about it.

BA: Well, he was always up for a bargain. And he would talk about even a suit of clothes: where he bought it and how cheap it was ten years ago somewhere. He'd found it at a sale or something, just an ordinary purchase. The cost would stick in his mind. He was very conscious of cost.

You talked about his feeling about show-offs, and it certainly applied to himself. He never was showing off. The two experiences on one of his Paris visits would be pertinent on that point. One was dinner at a little restaurant called the Soufflé, which was near my office on the Place de la Concorde. Someone there, obviously an American, recognized him, and, while nobody bothered him over dinner, when we finished and stood up to go, several people rose and started to clap. Presumably the French there didn't know him, but they rose and clapped, too. And Burger, obviously, was very, very pleased—as I think anybody should be—to have a dinner somewhere in Paris and be recognized and applauded just because you're there. He did acknowledge it with a little bowing and walked out very slowly and shook a couple of hands as they were offered as we went by. He obviously enjoyed it very much.

The second experience took place at the Louvre. When he

came to Paris, we always did at least one museum. On this occasion, we were at the Louvre. His favorites were the Impressionists. This day, we had wandered deeper into the Louvre and were walking along slowly at the point where the triangle has now been erected (the latest addition to the museum), and two American women (middle-aged) came up and asked, "Would you take a picture of us, please? We want a picture of us with the Louvre in the background." Warren said, "Well, I'll be very glad to oblige, of course."

I'm still in a dilemma as to whether I should have told them who was taking the picture. What I hoped was that they would go home and see a picture of him somewhere and realize who did them this favor. But, he didn't give me any kind of a gesture to introduce him. Anonymity was one of his joys, and he spoke of that when he came to visit us because he could move around without anybody recognizing him and without any kind of feeling of pressure or whatever. Of course, he moved very freely in the States, too. But he was nearly always recognized at home. So, afterwards, I said that maybe I should have told them who was taking their picture, and he said, "No, you did the right thing." But I still remember that, and I still kind of regret it because I think that, after the picture had been taken and we were moving off, I should have given them that little bit of excitement.

RT: Tell me about the Chief's manners.

BA: I've known two people who were distinguished by their sense of good manners (well, many more, but two who are really outstanding). One, of course, is Burger. The other was Ed Murrow. Never too little time for the proper greeting; never too little time for the thank you. And the proper farewell. Both were very, very meticulous in how they treated others.

RT: Do you recall the Chief's last business meeting in his chambers?

BA: The last group meeting on Bicentennial business was one with Frank Shakespeare, and of course you and me. It was on the subject of the Four Presidents Project. [We discussed adding a fifth President, George Bush, but were never able to bring it off owing to the Chief's ill health.] He never had another meeting.

RT: Who were the last ones to visit the Chief?

BA: You and I and Mike Luttig were about the three last ones outside the family, and of course you were in Michigan and Mike was very far away. I still remember what may have been our last somewhat coherent conversation. I came out; it was before noon, and I often did this to catch him over his breakfast. He was sitting there in his robe and pajamas, but not interested in talking. It was rather hard to sit there, but eventually I rose and took his hand and said, "Well, I've got to move on, Chief, but I'll be back soon." He had a good grip, so I said, "It's nice to see that you've still got that solid Burger grip." He kind of smiled. Then, as I was going out the door, he said something, and I didn't quite hear it. "What?" So the Korean maid/cook there (I forget her name) said, "He says you've got a good grip, too." That's the last full sentence he ever spoke to me.

We could reminisce forever as you say.

RT: There's no beginning, middle or end of this. From the time that you first met Burger in Minnesota, what kind of contacts did you have?

BA: I'd gone abroad as a foreign correspondent in '47, and it wasn't until '53 that both of us wound up here in Washington and very frequent contact resumed. I was assigned to Washington at the end of 1953 or in '54 from Germany, and he was here, of course, as Deputy or Assistant Attorney General. I was with my parents up in Grantsburg, Wisconsin. I wanted to have a long visit with them because they were growing old, and their fiftieth wedding anniversary was coming up. I had a call from Burger, who said approximately the following: "You know, Harold Stassen is running for the presidential nomination again, trying to stop Taft among other things, and still opposing the conservatives. The Ridder people (*St. Paul Pioneer Press and Dispatch*) want to help out. They want to do it by buying some articles signed by Stassen on current policies, and I just don't have time to write them, and I'm wondering if you'd write them?" I said, "Sure. I owe Harold a lot and probably you as well, and I'll do whatever you want me to do. I've got some time here." So he gave me five subjects, and I sat down and wrote five articles. I knew their policies well enough, so I didn't have to get any direction; they were all fine and they were all run in the *St. Paul Pioneer Press* and other Ridder papers. The Ridders paid him a lot of money and Burger sent me what was somewhat more than a token check, but not much more. In any event, I felt fully recompensed because I intended to do it for nothing. That's the kind of thing that you do for friends.

RT: Burnett, you have demonstrated your loyal friendship in countless ways.

BA: It's been real fun and constructive.

CHAPTER 11

INTERVIEW WITH
JUDGE J. MICHAEL LUTTIG

Judge J. Michael Luttig is presently U.S. Circuit Judge, U.S. Court of Appeals, Fourth Circuit, to which he was appointed on August 2, 1991. Previously, he was Aide to the Supreme Court of the U.S., 1976-1978; Assistant Counsel, Office of the Counsel to the President, The White House, 1981-1982; law clerk to the Honorable Antonin Scalia, U.S. Court of Appeals for the District of Columbia Circuit, 1982-1983; law clerk to the Honorable Warren E. Burger, Chief Justice of the U.S., 1983-1984; Special Assistant to the Chief Justice of the U.S., 1984-1985; Davis Polk & Wardwell, Washington, D.C., September 1985-1989; Principal Deputy Assistant Attorney General, Office of Legal Counsel, U.S. Department of Justice, March 1989-1990; Counselor to the Attorney General of the U.S., 1990-1991; and Assistant Attorney General, Office of Legal Counsel, U.S. Department of Justice, 1990-1991.

RT: When did you first meet the Chief?

ML: Ron, it was in 1976. When I graduated from college, I went into the Ford White House, working with Dave Gergen, who was then Communications Director. I had the intention of staying through the election and, if Ford were reelected, to remain. But at the same time that I had applied for this position at the White House, I had also submitted an application at the Supreme Court, with the judicial intern program. I was selected to that, and it was something of a dilemma for me, because I was working in the White House but had an opportunity to go to the Supreme Court. So I called my dad and said, "What should I do?" He said, "Well, frankly, everything that you've ever believed in and everything that you want to be is at the other end of Pennsylvania Avenue, and you should take that job." So, in—I believe it was September of 1976—I began working at the Court for what was a stint of two-plus years.

RT: Working with the Chief?

ML: Working with the Chief, and with Mark Cannon. Initially, more with Dr. Cannon or with the Chief's Administrative Assistant. Then, it was really through Dr. Cannon's good offices that I became introduced to the Chief and began working closely with him on his administrative work. Then, gradually, we began to travel together.

RT: Your relationship with the Chief lasted for 20 years. How would you characterize your ongoing relationship with him?

ML: I think that, as with any relationship, the nature of it changed over time. But that is especially the case when the young person has a relationship with someone older, like the Chief Justice— not only in age, but also in terms of his station in life. When I began with the Chief in '76, I was 22 years old and he was the Chief Justice of the United States. A man who was 70-plus years old. And I would do anything and everything he said to do when he said to do it. I was appropriately scared. And extremely respectful, if not reverential. Then, over time, the relationship changed, because when we began to travel there was a friendship, but only the kind of friendship that one of 22, 23, or 24 can have with someone who is 75. I was more than appreciative of even that, but I wouldn't want to overstate the nature of the friendship coming from his direction. But then over time—I came back to clerk with him years later—at that point it changed into a more intense professional relationship because I was working with him day to day on the law.

Then, in 1978, the Chief said to me, "Look, Mike, you want to be a lawyer, and to do that, you've got to go to law school. It's awfully tempting for you to remain here, both for me but also for you. On the other hand, I have an obligation to you, and I think you need to go to law school and get started." And I said, "Well, Chief, I don't really know how these things work, but I'm excited and ecstatic that I'm here." And he said, "Well, if you go to a place close, like the University of Virginia, you could continue to work with us here at the Court, both in spare time and in the summers." So that's basically what happened: I went to the University of Virginia, and then in the spare time and in the summers I would work with him and with the Court.

In 1977, the Chief Justice and Mrs. Burger and Mark and Mrs. Cannon and I went to the Soviet Union. The Chief Justice had been asked to come to the Soviet Union by President Brezhnev. It was very interesting because, from a historic standpoint, it was a time when relations between the United States and the Soviet Union were quite chilly. In particular, then-Ambassador Malcolm Toon was having great difficulty even getting an audience with President Brezhnev. And yet, the President asked Chief Justice Burger to come over. So we all went to the Soviet Union for a week or so. During that period, we were escorted, as it were, around the Soviet Union by the Chief Justice of the Soviet Union, who was then, I think, Lev Smirnov.

At one point, interestingly, President Brezhnev wanted to meet with the Chief Justice alone. But the Chief Justice refused to meet with President Brezhnev unless Ambassador Toon would be permitted to join him. That was the Chief's contribution to the geopolitical developments of that day. And I think in retrospect it probably turned out to be a fairly significant meeting, because here's the Chief Justice of the United States who didn't technically have any kind of diplomatic power but he was going to shoe-horn in the Ambassador to see President Brezhnev. That was his way of saying, "You will deal with our official representatives, and I will not see you alone." This was very, very important to the Chief. There was a long period during our stay in which it was unclear whether Brezhnev was going to accept the meeting upon those terms. Finally, though, we got the word that he would see Chief Justice Burger and that Ambassador Toon would be allowed to join him.

When I was in law school there was a reciprocal visit here by Chief Justice Smirnov, and Chief Justice Burger asked me to escort Chief Justice Smirnov and his delegation around the United States. The cities that we visited—I can't remember all of them— were New York City, Washington, D.C., Charlottesville, Chicago and Salt Lake City. The point of the story is that I joined the Chief in '76 as a judicial intern. I segued into a judicial aide position in which I continued to work with him administratively but began to travel with him a good deal, going to Finland and all over the United States. Then after going to law school in Charlottesville, I continued to work with him and did things like escort Chief Justice Smirnov around.

By the way, as I backtrack, in terms of a vignette, when there was a dispute resolution conference in New York sometime in 1976 or '77, I went with the Chief to that. My family came to New York at the same time; they had business there. They brought with them the girl that I was dating who, today, is my wife. I would have been 22 or 23 years old. But I was so intent on this opportunity that I had with the Chief Justice that there was nothing that could distract me from it. Never. Not sports, not extracurricular activities, not a social life, not the girl I was dating, nothing—because I recognized the opportunity that this represented. I'm from a family that had no political connections, nor the kind of money that could introduce you into these kind of circles. So for me to be there was no small matter. But here I was in New York City, with the Chief Justice, and my family was there with my girlfriend.

One night after wherever we had traveled—I was an aide de camp, you get the principal into the room, located for the night, and then you're free. So about ten o'clock, I said good night to the Chief and left the hotel. I met my girlfriend downstairs and said, "Let's just go out and grab a bite to eat." Goodness, she must have been 18, 19, or 20, and she was mortified that we might be seen together in New York City by the Chief Justice. As cautious as I was, I thought the odds of this were zero. So we took off walking down the street in New York City. We went to a restaurant, got a table by the window, and started to chat about the day. No sooner had we ordered, when I looked up, and here came the Chief Justice walking down the street of New York. He had obviously decided that he wanted to take a walk. I said to

Elizabeth, "Look, don't be nervous, but the Chief Justice is out and about; and I see him outside." She froze. And here came the Chief, and he came right by our window and passed us, and I said, "Well, everything's fine. We're in New York City, for goodness sake. There's no possible way that we would, by happenstance, run into each other." Well, I turned around, and the Chief Justice entered the restaurant. I said to Elizabeth, "The odds have come to pass at least that he's in the restaurant. But there's no way that he'll see us." My girlfriend and now wife was speechless. I mean, she just thought that this was the end of the relationship and the end of my career. And a few moments later, the Chief Justice was standing at our table. He was just as relaxed and casual and warm as if he were my dad. I'll never forget it. That was essentially the first time that the Chief met Elizabeth.

After chatting for a while, he turned to her and shook his finger at her, and said, "Young lady, you be sure that he gets to bed on time tonight. We have a busy day tomorrow." From that point forward, the Chief and Elizabeth were very close friends.

RT: I would speculate that you were probably the Chief's favorite clerk. You were with him for 20 years. You chaired the April 30, 1996, memorial tribute. You gave the principal eulogy at his funeral. You were the executor of his estate. Can you give me any reason why I should not identify you as his favorite clerk?

ML: Apart from the fact that there's no possible way for anyone to know whether I was or not, no. There's no possible way to know. In fact, my best guess is that the Chief wouldn't even know who his favorite clerk was. There's no question that we were close friends for a number of years. A lot of that is a product of the fact that I was in Washington and some large number of the clerks were not. So, I was available; I was accessible. In fact, I literally lived a mile or so down the road from him. As a consequence, many a night the Chief Justice would call and say, "I just closed my black notebooks for the day, and I'm going to take a walk. Why don't you come over, and we can take a walk?" Because I go to bed fairly early, it was not unusual at all for him to call *after* I was in bed and say, "Would you like to go for a walk?" This is kind of a funny story with my wife and family now, because without exception I would say, "Absolutely." He never asked me if I was in bed, and I never told him I was in bed. But I would get up, get dressed, drive to his house, have a cup of tea and walk around the neighborhood. It was that kind of opportunity, played over a period of time, that really gave me the chance to get to know him, and in turn, gave him the chance to get to know me. That's probably what accounts for the closeness.

RT: What was your relationship with the Chief in his final year?

ML: Over time, the relationship changed, and I was keenly conscious of the stages of the relationship. When we came into the years following his resignation from the Supreme Court, the character of the relationship changed from my standpoint in this way. I firmly believed that beginning at or about that period of time, I had this profound obligation to take care of him in the way that he had taken care of me when I was 20 years old. I didn't always want to spend every moment with him. I would have a social commitment that I would have preferred to go to, but it was at that stage of the relationship that I thought, "You know, this is when I repay the man for everything he's done for me."

In the final year, there were two to three times when those of us close to the Chief believed that he might be passing. There was one time, in particular, that I remember, because I was in Texas for the trial of one of the three kids who murdered my dad. I got a call from Wade, who said, "I just don't know whether my dad will make it through the night." There was this pit in my stomach, where you can't swallow, and the tears well up in your eyes, and I thought, "My God! This man who has been everything to me in my life may die without my being there." So traumatic was that thought for me that I called my secretary here in Washington, dictated a note to her, and had her go to the hospital that night with the note and give it to the Chief.

The exact substance of that note I can't recall now, but I know the essence of it. It was very direct. It was something like, "Chief, I understand that you're not feeling well. I just want you to know how much you mean to me." And I don't know, Ron, it's conceivable that at that point in the relationship—again, this was close to 20 years at that point—I may have said, "Chief, you know I love you." Because at that moment I thought that this could have been the good-bye. It turned out not to be.

Then as we proceeded throughout that year, I tried to go to the Chief's house regularly, three or four times a week for just a short visit. Of course, as we closed in on the day of his death, it was more and more painful for all of us, because he was not the man that we had seen or had worked with. To see a man of his strength and capacity become, in effect, an invalid was a very sad thing. But, again, in my own mind, the significance was that that was the very moment when I thought how much he needed me and the other friends he had. No matter how painful it was to us, we had an obligation to him at that point. In fact, after he passed away at the hospital, I was there literally 15 minutes or so later. As I recall, Burnett [Anderson] was there. When I got to the hospital, Wade had not arrived. I don't know if Burnett had been in with the Chief after his passing. I presume he had. I went in with the Chief and stayed by his side until Wade arrived.

I wanted to see that relationship through, so that that man would know how much he had meant to me.

RT: Once he was no longer Chief Justice he lost a lot of amenities.

ML: I think that all of us were concerned about that scenario. But on reflection, I don't know if that wasn't more over-reaction on our part because, as I said at the eulogy, and I believe this to my core, this was a very austere man. The trappings of the office never overwhelmed him in the way that the public, through the media, perceived. In the eulogy, the things I was referencing were the Rochester house. He lived on Rochester Street. This was the simplest of homes, very simply furnished. It was not elegant.

He was a product of his Minnesota roots. And I truly, truly believe that he never forgot those roots.

There was a kind of re-characterization of the man by the media. But at bottom, none of this mattered one whit to him. You and I talked earlier about how frugal he was: he would not spend a penny more for something than he thought it was worth. Now, I did for him as we all do with our grandparents—you see something that they want, and it's more than they are ever going to pay, but the price is clearly reasonable by today's standards. You or I would do anything we could to get it for them, and never even tell them the difference. You're talking about a man who was very, very frugal.

RT: Is there any comment that you want to make on his concept of public service?

ML: Two fundamental points come to mind. The first is that he believed in public service from the beginning, and to the end. Philosophically, he was an entrepreneur, yet he believed in public service. The second is that he truly believed that he was merely holding his office in trust for the public. He believed that countless other people literally could have held the office of Chief Justice just as effectively, if not more effectively, than did he. And in some way, that's the most revealing part of the man. He didn't think that he was chosen by the Divine to do this.

I have always thought that one of the most significant observations about the man is that he relinquished the most powerful judicial office in the world, and he did not do this after wringing his hands and going through a tremendous emotional upheaval. Why? Because he knew that he could do any of 20 or 30 other things that he had always wanted to do in life. Without naming names, he would often comment with respect to other members of the Court that the reason they stayed is because they believed—rightly or not—that they could do nothing else in life, and that once they left the Court, there was nothing left. That was just not his view. So the fact that he took over the Bicentennial was no surprise to any of us. In time, maybe he would have taken on something else, if only doing the artwork and the sculpting that he had wanted to do his whole life. He was a Renaissance man, in a way. He was a historian, he was a judge, he was a lawyer, he was an artist. He had a passion for politics, but yet he was much more.

RT: Anything you want to say about the Chief's attitude about kids, young people?

ML: I think I probably knew the Chief at a station in his life where insights into that part of him were few and far between. When I met him, his children would have been in their 40s and 50s, I believe. I do know that he loved the children of the clerks. Not only when they were young; he followed their careers as they went along. And my daughter, who is now only seven, knew the Chief, knows him, and as far as she knows, he's still alive.

RT: Did you ever hold any surprise parties or events for him?

ML: I'm not a very social person, in the sense of social activities. I'm a people person, but I'm not a social person. So it would not have been in my nature to hold a surprise party for him, although I was at his tenth anniversary surprise party at the Court and still have the orange and white placard that says "Chief" that we held up as he came in the conference room.

There was one surprise event that comes to mind. But it's not of the kind you're talking about. Elizabeth and I would spend a lot of our social time with the Chief and Mrs. Burger, and we would go to dinner on the weekends or during the week with frequency. One time, the Chief invited us for dinner on Saturday night. Elizabeth and I dressed up, got a bottle of wine, went over to his house (this was when he was in the townhouse on Wakefield) and knocked on the door. The Chief came to the door in his terrycloth robe. Well, I mean, we just went ashen, because it was clear to us that there had been a miscommunication somewhere, but we didn't know where. I will always have my guess. The odds that he could get confused on something like that were a lot greater than that someone at our station in life would be confused as to when the Chief Justice of the United States invited us to dinner. But, be that as it may, faced with the Chief there, I said, "Chief, Elizabeth and I were just heading downtown, and we thought we would just drop off this bottle of wine so you could chill it for our dinner tomorrow night." He said, "That's just tremendously thoughtful of you, and we are looking so forward to it," and closed the door, and that was it. My wife and I ate at Burger King that night, and then went with the Chief and Mrs. Burger the next night.

RT: Can you convey any stories about his ability to work with ordinary people?

ML: Yes, I think that that takes you back, really, to his roots. This is a man who grew up, probably not in poverty, but certainly not in affluence. He worked his way through college and law school and never had much. And as a public servant for so many years, he didn't have much, professionally. I think that he was, in many ways, a man of the people who was thrust into a position in which it's very difficult to be a man of the people. I think that's why we saw him spend so much time gardening, for instance. All of the clerks have their gardening stories, but we would get out and work the garden, work in the yard, plant and dig, and mow. He was quite, quite comfortable doing that. And he was as comfortable in informal clothes as he was in a suit or in the robe. But once you're elevated to that high office, the opportunities that you have are so limited. That's the trouble. That's not to say that he wouldn't have preferred to do it. As Clarence Thomas said during his hearings, he would much prefer to have been at Wal-Mart or at the grocery store or mowing his yard. I, frankly, have always thought the Chief would have been just as happy doing those same things.

RT: Burnett Anderson said that the Chief worked hard at keeping friends. He didn't take them for granted. How did that manifest itself with you or with others?

ML: I always believed that once he became a judge, but certainly after he became Chief Justice, that there was a certain inherent difficulty in acquiring new friends—because he just didn't know whether they had an agenda, or if they were trying to get something from him. So I think what he did was husband the friends that he did have, and treasure them more than he would have had he not held those positions. This was a man, who—in contrast to myself, for instance—was a very social person, in the sense that he enjoyed going to the cocktail party, or the reception, or the event, at the same time that he was intensely private. He moved so comfortably in a crowd. He probably worked the crowd, as it were, better than any politician that I've ever seen. And it was so natural, and so comfortable, and so easy for him. At the same time, he wasn't baring his soul to all these people. Very few people got to know him at all.

RT: Are there any pet peeves of his that you would feel comfortable in citing?

ML: Certainly, lawyer advertising was important to him. The profession of lawyering, and of judging, in particular, were almost sacred to him. He was never comfortable with the ethical developments that occurred during his lifetime. In terms of pet peeves, you catch me a little off-guard.

RT: What about public misconceptions of the Chief: What do you think they were and why?

ML: I alluded to one of them which was because he was, as they said, out of "central casting." He looked the part of the Chief Justice, and I'm unprepared to say that that's irrelevant. He had the bearing and the presence to be Chief Justice. But he felt so passionately about his obligations to that office, and, of course, to the public through that office, that the misimpression grew that he was caught up in the trappings of the office. As I said, I don't think he ever was caught up in the trappings of the office. There is a certain extent to which, after you've had a car for 15 years, that it becomes natural for you. But that's not the same as to say that you believe that you should have a car. As a practical matter, it really became over time more that he didn't know *how* to drive. If you haven't driven for 15 or 20 years, you don't know how to drive. And that's why he wanted the car, I think, for the Bicentennial Commission. I think to some degree that he almost became a man who was trapped in his office, as it were. He couldn't be himself except with a small circle of friends. And I think that that's a sad function of the office. It's not unlike the presidency in the sense that wherever you go, someone is watching.

RT: Any stories about his diplomacy?

ML: This gets into something that I, again, alluded to in the eulogy— that it's very easy at this point to criticize the Chief Justice for not pulling together a consistent majority at the Supreme Court of the United States. What we've lost sight of is that when he took office as Chief Justice, the institution itself was under almost merciless attack, and its credibility with the public was almost as low as it had ever been. His job over the next 15 years was to bring that entire institution to the forefront of public attention, and leave the institution with the public having the profound respect for it that it should. And he did that. That in itself is an accomplishment of diplomacy.

But within that task, and this is again something I alluded to and that people either ignore or don't have the tools to appreciate, he had, as Chief Justice, as diverse a set of personalities with him on the bench as perhaps one could ever have. You had during his tenure a William O. Douglas, a Thurgood Marshall, a Harry Blackmun, a William Rehnquist, a Byron White, a Sandra O'Connor. These are very, very different personalities, and they run the gamut in terms of jurisprudence. So to work with all those personalities and philosophies over a period of 15, 16, 17 years, at the same time that you are trying to renew the public respect of the Supreme Court, was, in my view, no mean feat at all. And I truly believe that this accomplishment is ignored by the commentators.

RT: Any stories about his sense of good manners?

ML: We're talking about a man of supreme etiquette and manners. He was as graceful, socially, as any man I've ever encountered. That's not to say that he knew every step as to how the place setting should appear. But in terms of grace, he was the epitome. I will add this interesting story that also sheds some light on the Chief. He was European in many ways. But he never, never questioned the values of the United States. I think he was just tempted more by the history of Europe. But that's too grandiose a way into this following vignette.

My family, at the time, had a place in Charlottesville, Virginia. When Chief Justice Smirnov [of the Soviet Union] came to the United States, he and the Chief stayed there. During one of their stays, I went to the kitchen late at night and the Chief had all this food laid out, including raw eggs cracked and in a saucepan to be fried. I said, "My goodness, Chief, are you going to have a late-night snack?" He said, "No, I just want to be ready in the morning for Chief Justice Smirnov." And as I am sitting here, the eggs stayed out all night already cracked, in the pan, to be fried.

I also give you a vignette that is certainly not positive about *my* etiquette or manners, but does shed a whole lot of insight into him. When we went to the Soviet Union, all of the meals were splendid, because, after all, he was the Chief Justice. One morning, however, at breakfast, they served hardboiled eggs in hardboiled egg cups. I had grown up in Texas and certainly had not been in the social circles that the Chief had. I had no idea what this was. The Chief took his knife and just clipped the top off that egg as if the egg had been perforated around the top. I then proceeded to beat my egg to a pulp, not knowing how to get the top of it off. Finally, with all the guests around, the Chief just called the maitre d' over and said very quietly so that no one else could hear, "Would you just bring my friend another egg?" They brought me another egg, and the Chief took the top off it for me.

One of the Chief's favorite stories out of that trip to the Soviet Union was this. I don't drink, and never have. But, of course, we were in the Soviet Union, where vodka was served all the time. There was an expectation that you would drink vodka with the Soviets. But I never did, of course. One night at one of the state dinners, I was occupying my fairly inconspicuous place at the table. I had made friends with all of our Soviet hosts. The Soviet Chief Justice stood up and toasted me, which surprised everyone, not least of whom, me. At the end, he said, "The only thing that we here in the Soviet Union don't understand is why young Luttig does not drink our vodka." There are no words for how scared I was. I was just grateful to be in the room at the table, but to be engaging the Chief Justice of the Soviet Union in the presence of the Chief Justice of the United States was more than I could handle. The Chief looked over at me and nodded as if to say, "You're expected to say something." So, I stood up, and all this being done through translators, said, "Mr. Chairman, thank you for your kind remarks. With respect to the question you asked, I would only say that I would be glad to drink with you, but my mother won't let me." As this came through the translator, the entire table of 30 or 40 people doubled over laughing and as they did, the Soviet Chief Justice raised his glass to me. The Chief told that story almost until his final day.

RT: Would you say that his character was complex or enigmatic in any way?

ML: I don't know that I would say it was complex. I probably would say that it was enigmatic. I think that, in many ways, with the Chief, you got what you saw. I don't think he ever played games. There was not another personality there. I always believed that the misperception came about because people projected onto the man something that was never him. And the "enigmatic" comes about because he never really was who they thought he was. He was just himself.

RT: Would you want to characterize what you think were the perceptions of liberals about him, and the perceptions of conservatives
about him?

ML: I'll take a stab at that. You've got the juxtaposition of the Warren
court era with the Burger court era. You have Burger's appointment by President Nixon under a law and order banner, so right
off, you have the expectation that he will be, at least by comparison, conservative. I think that, undoubtedly, by comparison, he
was conservative. I also believe that, if you artificially divided
the world into conservatives and liberals, he would be a conservative as opposed to a liberal. However, this was a very, very
moderate man. He would be extremely moderate by today's standards. In a sense, he was a man for the time.

On the specific question of what each camp would think of
him, the answers to that question are fairly obvious. Liberals
viewed him as very conservative and far to the right. But because of such decisions as *Roe* and *Swann against Charlotte-
Mecklenburg*, the conservatives never viewed him as particularly
conservative. I believe that as far as he was concerned, he was
steady throughout his whole career. He probably would have
characterized himself as conservative, but I think he was moderate to moderately conservative. You can't ignore or deny the
Minnesota roots. This is a man who had the greatest respect in
the world—not only professionally but politically and philosophically—for tradition. But this man was innovative. He was willing to experiment. He was not stodgy, he was not a stuffed-shirt.
He was willing to try anything in order to achieve something
better. If it didn't work, fine. But he was willing to try. That
often was what would distinguish him.

RT: It was my understanding that when he had polio he would lie in bed because he had to and would read the founding fathers and history. Was that your understanding?

ML: Yes. As I said in the eulogy, he had this uncanny sense that he had known the founding fathers. He read the original papers regularly and studied them. But I don't know that he would really consider himself an originalist. I suspect he would not. He was what I call a conventional jurist. He was case-law driven.

RT: You mean originalist in the sense of getting back to the original intention of the founders?

ML: Yes, or being held only to that. That was not him. That was just not him. He was first, and foremost, pragmatic. "Pragmatic" is the word that really captures not only the man, *qua* man, but the man, *qua* judge.

RT: Except he would not like it's being defined as a living Constitution, would he? That suggests it changes with the times. To say he's not an originalist would not necessarily mean that he was in favor of the so-called living Constitution concept that you can just change the Constitution at will to fit the times.

ML: That's certainly true, but the enterprise that he engaged in was not different in kind but more in degree. His was the common-law approach of incremental change. But to the extent that a living Constitution meant something volatile and dynamic day to day, that was not his view.

RT: Heavy reliance, then, on the tradition of the past as it evolved?

ML: Yes. I learned first with him, and then through Justice Scalia, the passion for case law. That's what you work from, existing case law, in his instance, that of the Supreme Court.

RT: There's got to be precedent. But precedent can change.

ML: Precedent can change. And, of course, he above all was comfortable with change—just incremental. He believed that the system and humanity were fallible, and he expected that. And he thought that was good and natural. But if you move incrementally, then the affirmative harm that is done is not that great.

RT: I have one of the draft papers he sent me, and I don't know that it was ever published, where he was attempting to deal with the matter of gun control as he perceived the founders to have thought about it.

ML: Let me make this observation. With respect to that particular issue, the case law is so scant that there is almost no resource to turn to, but the original understanding.

RT: Do you have any of his artwork? I see you have the Dante death mask.

ML: Here at the office I have the literary map of England that he did when he was at Johnson High School. He received an A+.

RT: He told me once that for blacks there ought to be special consideration simply because, unlike Hispanics, women, gays, you name it, blacks were brought to this country against their own volition. Because of that, he said we have an obligation to them. Now you can agree or disagree with that, but you know at least where he's coming from.

ML: It doesn't surprise me, because the line that he used in his own mind was never as stark and impenetrable as people who, without a knowledge of him or even his cases, thought. For instance, he has, by jurisprudence, some of the most expansive First Amendment and First Amendment press cases on the books. No one gives him credit for that, because they have decided that he didn't like the media in general. Now, whether that's true or not, let's assume that it was for purposes of our discussion here. The fact that he was able and willing to write those opinions speaks volumes about the man as a jurist. He was not importing his personal views into the Constitution. Now, just by way of an aside, the perceived view by the media that he did not *respect* the media was not even correct.

RT: Do you know of any examples where his personal feelings or emotions were at odds with the Constitution, but he always let the Constitution triumph? He told me that he didn't like capital punishment, but would defer to the Constitution which permits it. Was there anything else where emotionally or personally he felt one way but would move in a different direction?

ML: There was no question that the Chief had at least an ambivalence toward the Washington media. I'm not so sure it was toward the national media. Again, his First Amendment jurisprudence was expansive in favor of press rights. But as to the capital punishment area that you identify, that was unquestionably true. And I knew that, and without a doubt. Other areas? I don't think the Chief had a Second Amendment case at all. But you're familiar with the story that got a lot of negative publicity for him when he opened his door at home at ten o'clock or so at night with a gun in hand.

RT: Can you describe for me your last meeting with the Chief?

ML: He was in a hospital bed—and had been for a while—in his bedroom on the second story of the townhouse. I would take an interesting article from the newspaper that day, or something, to make conversation with him. He was largely non-responsive so that, when I left, he would just nod acknowledgment of his appreciation and his awareness that I was there—and would cry. I would say to him, "Chief, you're the strongest man that I've ever known. This will not get the better of you. You will come through this just fine." But the truth of the matter is, and I think all of us knew this, after Mrs. Burger died, as is often the case, it was never the same for him.

RT: Did he die of congestive heart failure, or was it pneumonia?

ML: I don't know what the recited or medical cause of death was. But my lay view, and nothing more than that, is that he just died of old age. Things just began to quit.

RT: I used to watch him eat eggs and butter and bacon, and I would say, "How can you eat so much of that stuff?" And he said, "My cholesterol and my blood pressure don't even register."

ML: He loved to eat. And he loved my wife's cooking. He loved her lasagna. He loved good, heavy food. When we would go to the country club down the road, where he ate often with Mrs. Burger, and where he ate often especially after she died, he would always get a big steak, baked potato, that kind of thing. It didn't seem to bother him. He was never really overweight or too heavy. He walked and exercised quite a bit.

As we were talking, one thing that came to mind was that I

was with the Chief when he was building the townhouse. He was as excited about that as anything I had ever seen. He would go out to the townhouse at least twice a day, in the morning and the evening, if not more. And he would essentially supervise the construction of that townhouse. If he found a wall that had been erected where he didn't think it should be, he would just write across the face of the wall, "MOVE THIS WALL!" with an exclamation mark. I would have hated to be the contractor on the house! But you can be assured of one thing: before it was over, that house was what he wanted it to be. And that's the way he did much of his life.

This was a very, very warm, natural man who had a passion for life. He had an energy for life that could be unparalleled. He knew politics from the '40s and '50s forward—seemingly congressional race by congressional race and presidential election by presidential election. He had a command over politics. He loved it. But he also had a rather deep understanding of international affairs. Yet, at the same time, he loved gardening and art.

RT: And he liked Hubert Humphrey, and at the same time when he was in Minnesota, he was the one who organized and helped get William Buckley to speak there.

ML: I actually think that that is not so difficult to understand if you understand from whence he came, and realize that he was then placed in a position from which it was difficult for others to have a close, first-hand understanding of the man.

I just want you to know, whatever the purpose of this taped interview is, that I owe everything to that man. It's not just that I wouldn't be sitting here today as a judge. I would have been nothing, professionally, without that man. And I'll stand beside him for the rest of my life. And I don't care who his critics are. That's not to say that I agreed with everything that he said, but I do tell you this: I owe everything to Warren Burger. And, he knew that I believed that. And he never asked for anything in return.

Chapter 12

Interview with
Judge Kenneth W. Starr

Judge Kenneth W. Starr joined Kirkland & Ellis in February 1993 and was appointed Independent Counsel on the Whitewater matter in August 1994. From May 1989 to January 1993, Mr. Starr served as Solicitor General of the United States, where he argued 25 cases before the Supreme Court involving a wide range of governmental regulatory and constitutional issues of commercial importance. Prior to taking the oath of office as Solicitor General, he served as a United States Circuit Judge, having been appointed to the United States Court of Appeals for the District of Columbia Circuit in October 1983. In January 1981, Judge Starr became Counselor to United States Attorney General William French Smith, a position he held until his judicial appointment. He practiced law in Los Angeles and Washington, D.C. with the firm of Gibson, Dunn & Crutcher, where he was a partner in litigation practice. Previously, Judge Starr served as a law clerk to U.S. Court of Appeals Judge David W. Dyer (1973-74) and to Chief Justice Warren E. Burger (1975-1977). Judge Starr was admitted to the California Bar in 1973. Subsequent Bar admissions include the Virginia Bar in 1979, District of Columbia in 1979, and the U.S. Supreme Court in 1989.

I once had to introduce Judge Starr at a Bicentennial function. He was the representative on Bicentennial matters for the Second Circuit Court of Appeals in Washington. In preparation for the introduction I asked the Chief, "If you were limited to just one observation about Ken Starr, what would it be?" He thought for some moments, then said, "He can disagree without being disagreeable."

RT: When did you first meet the Chief?

KS: I actually met the Chief after I was on the job, so I had not met him prior to beginning my clerkship. I met him very shortly thereafter in July 1975. The Chief used a screening committee, and at the time that my application was being considered, I was on the West Coast. While I think he may have interviewed certain persons, I was actually interviewed in the screening process by one of his former law clerks, Reese Bader, who was and continues to be on the West Coast. I was hired sight unseen. I did have one telephone conversation with him when he was kind enough to offer the clerkship, and I accepted; but I was in Los Angeles and he was in Washington.

RT: You were appointed for two terms. Isn't that unusual?

KS: Well, I was actually appointed for one but was asked to remain on. The Chief and I joked about it: that I didn't graduate with my class, that I was a bit of a slow learner and had to be left behind to learn to do it right. I can augment that because it goes to the Chief's interest in judicial administration, which was, of course, such a keen interest of his. Justice [Lewis] Powell came to the Court in the early 1970s. Having come from a large law firm, in contrast to the background of most of the Justices, Justice Powell was rather accustomed to a number of young lawyers junior to him assisting in his cases. He felt then, given the workload of the Court, that having three law clerks was insufficient. So the Chief had an experiment. Our first year (my first term at the court, which was in 1975), Justice Powell had four law clerks. The Chief Justice of the United States historically had four during Chief Justice Warren's era when certain responsibilities fell to the Chief's chambers, with respect to what we call the IFPs (*in forma pauperis* petitions for review, filed by indigent persons). The Chief dispensed with those duties, so, when I was there, there were only three law clerks.

During the course of that Term, the Chief [Burger] decided, possibly in consultation with the Conference, that he would go to four law clerks the following term, and he was kind enough to ask me to remain on to provide a certain amount of continuity; so I remained on for two terms.

RT: What was the nature of your continuing relationship? I'd mentioned to you earlier that if one were to pick a short list of his friends, you were certainly on that list.

KS: Well, I was very fortunate that I left in '77. About that time, Judge [Griffin] Bell was very much ensconced as the Attorney General of the United States, and I had come into Judge Bell's orbit; so there were a few ways in which I—even though I was in private law practice—sort of floated around some of the issues. I knew a lot of people in the Bell Justice Department, and the Chief was interested in the Williamsburg Conference, among other things, that your predecessor, Mark Cannon, had been involved in. But I would say that in those years immediately after the departure, I did not have an especially close (day-to-day or week-to-week) relationship, but my closeness to Judge Bell (my having clerked in the old Fifth Circuit) helped pave the way so that I was fortunate enough to be asked by William French Smith to serve as his counselor and Chief of Staff. One of my official responsibilities was dealing with judiciary issues on behalf of the Attorney General. I was very fortunate to have reason to be involved with the Chief Justice and the Chief Justice's work by virtue of my own continuing public service, and we continued to see one another.

I was always the subject of the Chief Justice's good humor. By virtue of his keen interest in the Justice Department, he treasured those days of his at the Justice Department serving under General Brownell, then General Rogers, then on to the Court of Appeals, then back to Minnesota, and then finally Vera's less-than-robust health guiding him to remain here, with no intention of going on the bench. He loved to tell stories. I loved to sit at his feet, so to speak, for those stories and would be a more than receptive audience just because of my following in his footsteps at the Justice Department. He loved the Justice Department.

At that time in particular, he was goal-oriented; I mean he was very purposeful in his activity. Things were not random. He had catholic interests, to be sure, but he was goal-oriented, without saying, "I am goal-oriented." Everything was purposeful and pointed in a sort of teleological way toward some end; and with my having grown up, with his helping raise me, so to speak, in his chambers for two years, I came to really love and deeply admire him, and his work caused me to take a particular interest in his projects: the Williamsburg seminar, trying to work for his judges (and he viewed them as his judges) around the country, working for judicial survivors benefits and compensation increases. He hated to see judges leave the bench because of financial circumstances. We worked collaboratively, and of course I was staff; so I worked with Mark Cannon and others, but I would be able to rub shoulders with the Chief by virtue of that. That was throughout the '80s. I was fortunate enough to go on to the bench, and he could not have been more gracious, more supportive, in very helpful ways that I'm not even sure of. I wish I knew. He helped behind the scenes, in terms of my own judge-ship. Not that the Chief was *deus ex machina*, but he certainly was working, appropriately, behind the scenes to be of help to Ken.

RT: What was your relationship with the Chief in his final year?

KS: I would say that I tried to be dutiful as we former clerks were trying to encourage him to carry on, to make sure that he knew that we cared for him, that we wanted him to take care of him-self. And I tried to be supportive by personal visits. The last time I was with him was at the hospital, but he did not want to see anyone. He was not feeling well at all. The last time that I saw him at his home was with Mike [Luttig], who was so dutiful. No one was more so than Mike. We had lunch with the Chief; Elizabeth [Luttig] had baked a lasagne, which was delicious, but the Chief just picked at his food.

RT: Any comments you want to make about the Chief's view on public service?

KS: The Chief was a great booster of public service. Even though he himself very much loved his experience in private life—we would hear charming stories of private law practice and clients and young lawyers trying cases in Minnesota—I would say, through his trum-peting of the joy and professional satisfaction that he had at the

Justice Department, that this is the good professional life. And I would say also that he would not put on a pedestal someone who, let's say, was a fabulously successful lawyer: "Oh, well, he's managing partner of law firm A, B, and C," in juxtaposition to someone who might be an assistant United States Attorney. So by his example and what he chose to highlight, the Chief would guide us somewhat indirectly, as opposed to saying, "You should go work at the Justice Department."

I would say, also—and this is somewhat off point, but I think it deserves mentioning—that he was practical and had such common sense. His were insights born of native intellect and the ability to see things so clearly. He could make interesting comparisons. For example, he would say to someone interested in teaching [law], "Would you want someone teaching surgery who had never performed an operation? Don't you think you should learn how to perform an operation before you go teach young surgeons how to perform surgery? By the same token, you should go practice law for a while before you teach." He had what he called the five-year rule: that no one should be teaching until he had five years of experience, which would include clerkships. "Be a clerk for two years; that's fine. Now, go practice law or do something before you report to teach." He was very fond of the teaching enterprise, but this was the mixture of his very practical, common-sense bent.

RT: Any anecdotes or stories about his sense of humor?

KS: I found his sense of humor to be situational. He didn't tell a lot of jokes, but he would have that little gleam in his eye and the little smile, and you knew that he was going to be teasing you in the most good-natured way. He was so free of malice and guile, which I think was very much not understood and unappreciated. I can't say his favorite story was one thing or other, because I don't think he had one, but his humor responded to the flow of events around him. He liked to poke fun good-naturedly at folks who might otherwise take themselves a little bit too seriously, but not in a malevolent way. He would love to poke fun at the big law schools, he having gone first to a small one.

RT: Any stories that you know about his ease in working with ordinary people?

KS: We had a wonderful person at the Court, and perhaps they are still called messengers. Our messenger was a very dear, dear man, an elderly African-American gentleman. Having served under another Chief, he was very admiring of the Chief [Burger] and the way the Chief was thoughtful, often caring about him. I recall the groundskeeper and housekeepers at the house before they sold the property on Rochester Street in Arlington. Both the Chief and Mrs. Burger were very dutiful toward them. Their daughter would continue to come over and look after the Chief and Mrs. Burger long after her parents had retired. I'm not going to say that they were family, but there was just a great warmth and caring. I think they were from the Philippines.

RT: Can you think of anything he did to keep you as a friend?

KS: I think I'd have to leave it to others because it was more for him to view me. I always viewed myself as so junior to him that I wouldn't say, "I'm the Chief's friend." I'm almost uncomfortable putting myself in the category of friend because I worked for the Chief. That was my job.

RT: Did you feel, even before he died, that it was still the relationship of the mentor and the pupil?

KS: Oh, yes. Absolutely, absolutely. He would continue to give me thoughtful guidance and advice.

RT: What was his relationship with Nixon and other Presidents?

KS: I can't comment on much other than to say that I think that he was impressed by President Carter. He had very kind words to say about President Carter early on in his tenure, which of course was late in my tenure. Here's someone from a completely different background, a different political party, although the Chief did not talk about things in partisan ways other than historically. He loved telling stories of Eisenhower and the work of the Minnesota Delegation. He never trumpeted his own role. He always tried to think well of people. He had a sort of Will Rogers aspect in him: "I never met a man I didn't like." He held President Ford in high regard. Above all, he loved his country, and he wanted to see Attorneys General do well, he wanted to see presidents do well, he wanted his judges to do well. He wanted them to have the tools they needed to do their jobs.

RT: Whatever party?

KS: Absolutely. He was very supportive of the President. He did not talk that much about Nixon around me. He had great admiration for Eisenhower, speaking always in tones of great and deep respect. But they would tend quickly to be combined: It wasn't Eisenhower standing alone as in some MacArthur-like figure larger than life.

RT: What do you think were the public misconceptions about the Chief? You've named one, that he was "heavy-handed." And you simply defined that as a form, really, of candor.

KS: Yes.

RT: Any other misconceptions when you think about the Chief?

KS: I think the thought was that he was pompous and arrogant. Maybe that is just a handmaiden of "high-handedness" and a certain "mean-spiritedness." I couldn't quite define the reasons for this, other than he didn't invite the press corps in for chummy-chats, and he wouldn't go palling around with them to baseball games. I think he was always being compared—unfavorably of course— in the press's mind to Earl Warren, who was viewed as a demi-god. Yet his basic warmth and humanity was manifest, day in and day out. I suppose part of the misconception is, it was so frequently said, that it looked as if the Chief were straight out of central casting, and I think his bearing, which was very impres-sive, conveyed to some, "Well, he's not one of the guys." Whereas Chief Justice Warren, I gather, could be like your uncle or your grandfather whose knee you'd climb on. The Chief had a certain dignity about him, and what a magnificent voice.

Another thing was his profound respect for other systems of law, especially his great love and admiration for the British sys-tem. He had keen interest in Scandinavian prisons and very keen interest (which I greatly admired) in reforming prisons into "fac-tories with fences." I viewed him as sort of Burkeian, someone who had a great sense of institutional and structural integrity, a sense of what the appropriate role was for the respective branches in our separation of powers system. But at the same time, he loved to reform institutions. "Let's make them better, but let's not do it in an illegitimate way." So his view was very much, "Let's play by the rules: we are not Leninists here. It is not, what is to be done and let's adjust ends and means." He was so deeply moral about right and wrong, and such a great respecter of our institutional arrangements, that he would never do what Chief Justice Earl Warren would do and declare like a judge sitting in equity what is right and then read the Constitution to achieve his own moral view of what is right under the circumstances. I think he was viewed as, frankly, a bit of an instrument of Nixonian regressivism/non-progressivism, but in fact, he was in the spirit of Holmes, of Frankfurter, of Harlan, and the like, jurisprudentially; but at the same time in contrast to those worthies, he was always out there voting with his feet, urging, for example, "Let's make this prison better." He would assert, "I have reservations about the death penalty, and I'm not sure I would vote in favor of it in the state legislature, but I don't have a shadow of doubt that the Constitution expressly mentions it."

RT: What impact did the Depression have on him?

KS: I can't say. I mean, he was always generous, he would always bring things in to us, so I never knew him to be anything other than wonderfully generous. What I found was that it ended up curbing certain opportunities that it was probably providential that he didn't have—for example, not to be able to go off to Princeton as he could have done, because he had to stay close to home. He came up the old-fashioned way: milk routes, paper routes, and the like. It gave him a grounding; if he had had his ticket punched in all of the right places, maybe he would have ended up being a very different kind of person. He admired hard work, and he was a prodigious worker. He'd always be saying, "You know, I was reading this book about . . . ." How did he do it? It was clear to me that he kept several books on his bedtime shelf. He would do nighttime reading, but I never saw him take an afternoon reading siesta. I think a lot of children of the Depression were very ardent about labor. I don't mean the trade movement. They were very ardent about working.

RT: Anecdotes or stories about his good manners?

KS: He was always unfailingly polite. He had a bit of the best of the old school. You had the sense that the Chief was proper, without being stuffy. I didn't think he was the least bit stuffy. Yet that was part of the atmosphere about him. For example, he would frequently use the last name [to address someone]—when I knew full-well that he knew the first name—just to make sure that he was being polite. Sort of English manners.

RT: Would you say that his character was complex or enigmatic?

KS: Not enigmatic. And I'm not even sure that it was complex in that I felt that the Chief was the quintessential middle American, with a European set of tastes. That is, he would enjoy a good German wine, or dealing with one judge or other. Yet at bottom he was just a solid son of the Middle West. So much of his education was by dint of his own labor.

RT: What do you think the liberals' views of him were, and then the conservatives'?

KS: Let me begin with the conservatives' because I'm not sure that I have thought adequately through the liberals' view beyond what I said: how can anyone replace the demigod [Earl Warren]? I think that the conservatives viewed him as being very much of a traditional justice who was seeking, case by case, to find the right answer. And he had certain, basic animating principles such as, and I would say most prominently as befits his beloved Constitution, his devotion to principles of separation of powers. I think those are of enduring significance in terms of his own jurisprudence. I think there was a sense among conservatives that he should have been more strongly moored in principle, so that a case like *Roe v. Wade* should never have been decided the way that it was, because it was constitutionally suspect; how could the Chief have signed onto the opinion? How could he have assigned it? Just how could we have gotten to where we got? And they had a sense that perhaps he did not have a particularly well-worked-out philosophy, save in separation of powers and in the criminal justice arena. I think conservatives would view criminal justice as a significant contribution on his part, very early on in his tenure, to limit the logical march of certain Warren Court decisions especially of the mid '60s. And I would say that he felt—this goes to first principles, and I guess I'm sensing this keenly these days, given my own activity now [in the President Clinton/Monica Lewinsky investigation]—such a profound respect for the eternal verities, including the importance of truth. He worked tirelessly for a few years in opposition to the Fourth Amendment exclusionary rule because it was an impediment to the truth-seeking process, but eventually it was just not to be. In several cases he would write very powerfully, and this came straight from the core of his thinking, that no one can commit perjury. And he had no tolerance for the excuse, "Well, I wasn't given certain warnings before I committed perjury." The idea of basic human responsibility and accountability, those things that we're now debating as a nation, to him were absolutely vital points. And I think conservatives appreciated that. Could he, however, overcome in their minds, in addition to *Roe,* cases such as *Swann v. Charlotte-Mecklenburg*, which ushered in busing, which was so disruptive? And I'm not sure that he could have, in conscience, decided the case differently because the law is subject to equitable discretion. And I think that thoughtful conservatives would look at him and say that he had to respect the prerogatives of district judges in these very sensitive social policy areas like desegregation. But at the same time, he would say, no extremes. He was somewhat of a centrist in that respect—less like Justice Scalia, more like Justice O'Connor—in that he would say, and I think the Detroit school desegregation litigation is a useful example of this, "All right, there is wide discretion that the district court has in bringing about desegregation, but you can't obliterate school district lines." That was his position on the *Milliken v. Bradley* litigation. So I think he achieved in part what President Nixon was hoping, that his Court was not going to continue to march down the road of criminal justice revolution. But there were other issues that were bubbling up: how were those to be handled? Eventually, I think—and this is what to me should historically stand the test of time—what ended up happening in the late '70s and '80s were the institutional arrangements: Congress's power, the power of the judiciary, and the power of the Executive Branch. That was one of his most enduring contributions; there, his rootedness is very appreciated by conservatives.

Liberals, I think, ended up coming to what I would call grudging respect for him from their perspective, if one assumes that liberals would say, "*Roe v. Wade* was rightly decided." They would appreciate that he was willing to move in a way that was not predictable for someone with his jurisprudential background. He was also a very unabashed defender of the First Amendment without, again, being extreme, arguing that there does have to be balance. I think liberals would also praise his vindication of religious liberty in *Yoder*, the Wisconsin Amish case. [This decision permitted the Amish to teach their children at home rather than be coerced into compulsory public-school attendance.] I would say there he showed this rootedness in the permanent things, in the idea that family should be able to be free of state intrusion in the rearing of children. But he ended up not engaging—and I think this is true in the affirmative action areas as well—in rigorous analysis, asserting, "All right, we're going to uphold *Fullilove v. Klutznick*. We're going to uphold in the *Fullilove* decision Congress' rather ham-handed attempt at affirmative action: a ten percent set-aside on a public works program. These are difficult questions, but we're going to defer to Congress." It was the theme of judicial restraint, but we're concerned about this. So I would say, with all due respect to my beloved Chief, that *Fullilove* was (and I think *Wisconsin v. Yoder* can be viewed this way as well) an understandable result, a sympathetic sort of judicial restraint, trying to respect Congress in one instance and trying to respect the right of families to rear their children in another. But it was jurisprudentially not as firmly rooted as I would have liked.

RT: He read prodigiously about American history.

KS: One of the things that he taught me, and he was the first person in my little world who did, was a sort of living history—not that he was living history, but that history was living in him. He had so steeped himself in the stories, the lessons and heroes of the past that they were almost like his friends. There was a flesh-and-blood nature to this; these were real human beings, and I learned mightily from that. I came to really *love* history through the Chief.

May I say one thing about the Chief as populist and the Chief as gentle teacher: gladly would he learn, and gladly teach. He believed that the Supreme Court itself should be a place of citizenry learning, with displays, the little movie theater, etc. He enabled a national history lesson and turned the Court into a citizen-friendly environment. Everybody says, "Oh, he was so efficient, always looking for efficiency, cutting down the length of arguments and so forth." Well, it was exactly the right thing to do. How much are you going to learn if you spend nine days on a case with people reading from dusty law books to Justices who should have already done their reading before they got on the bench? So his entire thrust was, "How do we make this building accessible? Let's use the building. Let's have the Supreme Court Historical Society. Let's make sure that our people know our history."

RT: Did he ever use the term "secular humanism"?

KS: I don't remember him using that. He tended not to use pejorative terms. He wasn't a big one for coining phrases; he spoke simply and didn't use a lot of fancy words, even though he had an elegance of expression. I always thought, "Oh, that'd make a good transcript." I'd just sit there and be entranced.

RT: The Chief's views on legal ethics?

KS: He felt that the legal profession had many baleful trends and tendencies, and he wanted to stand against them. His position on lawyer advertising showed his sense of the dignity of the profession. To him this was a grand and noble profession with a proud tradition, but those traditions were in jeopardy, demeaned by charlatans and ambulance chasers. The lack of integrity in the system, the idea that a judge could somehow be corrupt, was just utterly inadmissible. This was his grounding. This goes to the permanent things. He knew right from wrong. He was not, although he would never use these terms, a moral relativist. He would say truth is right; deceit and falsehood are wrong. You don't mislead the court, you don't mis-cite cases, and you don't lie and dissemble in your personal activities.

RT: Do you know of examples where his personal feelings and emotions were at odds with the Constitution, but he followed the Constitution?

KS: I think the clearest example is the death penalty. He never really opened up to me on his moral views on abortion, but I cannot help thinking, given his grounding, that he would think that abortion is morally wrong, but I don't know that.

RT: When was your last meeting with the Chief?

KS: My last actual meeting with him was at Sibley, a very few days before his death. He was clearly in discomfort, so I left the room. I saw him; we made eye contact. I could tell that he was not in the mood to talk. I don't know whether he recognized me; it was just sort of a nod of the head. So I waited outside. I went back into his room about half an hour later, and he was attending to personal matters. I'm afraid that the last time that I saw him was not memorable. The last time that I really saw him was at that lunch at his house when Mike Luttig and I were there really to encourage him to eat, and he wasn't talking very much. But I do have one anecdote from that.

I had recently taken on in my private practice the representation of the entire tobacco industry in a groundbreaking nationwide class action of literally tens of millions of persons. My representation entirely was whether this was a proper class action under Rule 23 of the Rules of Civil Procedure, and under the Constitution. The Chief was strongly anti-smoking long before it became fashionable to be anti-smoking. I didn't smoke, but he showed his disapprobation of my representing this industry. He looked at me, and I could tell he did not think one of his sons should be representing the tobacco industry. I said, "Chief, I'm not saying tobacco is good. This is the historic legal position. You don't approve of murder because you're representing the murderer. I don't buy the products, but the issue is, should this be a nationwide class action?"

RT: He wouldn't allow any of the constitutional programs at the Commission to be sponsored by the tobacco companies. And they tried. I got the feeling he more or less rejected them for their political baggage. What, he thought, would be the public criticisms of allowing tobacco companies to sponsor our events? I didn't see it necessarily as an objection to the fact that it was the tobacco people doing it, but rather to the perception they were doing it and that we would be criticized.

KS: He was ahead of his time, wasn't he?

RT: Please tell the story of the Chief taking his clerks to the hospital on the birth of your son.

KS: This was a very happy thing. Our child was still in the hospital. He had had a couple of complications, and Alice had as well. The Chief had gathered the clerks up to go to the City Tavern for lunch, and we were chatting. I said, "Well, I'm going to be heading back to the hospital this afternoon. Alice and the baby are doing fine." "Let's go," said the Chief. So off we went, impromptu, to George Washington Hospital. I'll always remember Alice saying, "Oh, I haven't done my hair." Our son was not with mom, so we went into the viewing room, and here's the Chief looking in at the babies, including mine. And it was a very sweet scene. It was just one of those impromptu things as opposed to, "Now, on today's agenda . . . ." It was the spontaneity about it that made us treasure it all the more.

RT: Is there anything else that's warm, touching, humorous, or embarrassing in good taste about the Chief?

KS: Yes. He was always hospitable, and I tried to convey this in my tributes. I can't say how much I appreciated then and treasure now those Saturday afternoons when he would do the cooking. I would be sitting there and saying, "Isn't this wonderful? You have really been blessed. How fortunate you are, and you should be down on your knees giving thanks, that with all these qualified people, many more qualified than you are, you are sitting here with the Chief Justice of the United States, in his little kitchen, carrying on a conversation with you and others, and he is fixing you soup on a Saturday afternoon." That was his way of taking us to the ballpark. He wasn't a big ballpark guy. But that was him. And I thought that was the essence of being in his chambers: a Saturday afternoon, quiet. It was a dress-down day.

I remember that he was very informal and warm and gracious. We would all sit around and there was a certain equality of the dining table. It was clear that he viewed us as his professional colleagues, not that we would put ourselves up there with him. He said in a tribute to Henry Friendly that as an advocate he showed respectful equality. It's like your "sweet majesty" quotation from *Henry V*: respectful equality. He had lifted that respect up to advocates. He was there, respectfully, to engage with them, they with him. In his view, there's no Uriah Heep-ish element. There's no reason to be obsequious. You respectfully assist them, and guide them, as your professional counterpart. And, in a way, he was evincing to us kids, who were wet behind the ears, that he was treating us with this kind of respectful equality of his little table in his inner office.

CHAPTER 13

INTERVIEW WITH
LLOYD N. CUTLER

Lloyd N. Cutler has been a partner in the Washington law firm of Wilmer, Cutler & Pickering and a predecessor firm from 1946 to 1979 and from 1980 to 1990. In 1991 he became Counsel to the firm and is now Senior Counsel. In 1979-80, and in 1994, he served as Counsel to the President of the United States. He has also served as Special Counsel to the President on Ratification of SALT II Treaty, 1979-1980; President's Special Representative for Maritime Resource and Boundary Negotiations with Canada, 1977-1979; Senior Consultant, President's Commission on Strategic Forces (Scowcroft Commission), 1983-1984; as a member of the Quadrennial Commission on Legislative, Executive and Judicial Salaries, 1985, and as Chairman, 1989; Member, President's Commission on Federal Ethics Law Reform, 1989; and as a consultant to Secretary Christopher and Ambassador Holbrooke during the Dayton negotiations, 1995.

RT: When we did our moot court case, you recall, I had been made the clerk of the court, and I was to give you all equal time. You may remember that Herb Brownell went way over the time. I tried to get him to stop, but he wouldn't pay any attention to me. I resolved that I would give you exactly the same time, and when it was over, the Chief said, with no animosity, "Didn't you give Lloyd extra time?" "Yes, Chief. I gave him exactly the same amount of time that Herb Brownell took." He didn't dispute that.

LC: He used to be more generous on time than Rehnquist is right now.

RT: Why do you think the Chief selected you as a member of our moot court team to England and Ireland from among the myriad of other attorneys and judges?

LC: Well, I imagine it was partly that I argued a number of cases before him. And we used to have lunch or dinner from time to time. We both shared an interest in wines, and you know what a great gourmand he was. And I helped him make up the [moot court] case. It was based partly on the Taiwan Defense Treaty case, *Carter against Goldwater*, and partly on a hypothetical derived from that. And when we put the case together, and I think I did some of this with Bob Clare, then I was invited to take part as one of the advocates. But whether Clare was the one who proposed me, or whether the Chief thought of it himself, I don't know.

RT: Why do you think he chose that particular case?

LC: It was such an interesting case, I think. He had been involved in the Court that decided *Goldwater against Carter*, in which there was no majority opinion. There were several plurality opinions, but basically, it turned on the Court saying this is a political question. We won't resolve it. And the fascinating case would be, since the Senate can ratify a treaty with conditions or reservations, suppose the Senate ratified a treaty with a reservation that if the President exercised the withdrawal clause of the treaty— almost every treaty has one for supervening events—that he would first have to get the consent of the Senate in order to withdraw. It's very much like the basic issue in the Andrew Johnson im-

peachment. That is, could Congress say that the President cannot remove a confirmed member of the Cabinet, except with the
further consent of the Senate? It's that kind of case. And there
were one or two Supreme Court precedents that came close to
the issue, but had never resolved it. So it was a wonderful case,
in that sense, to debate.

RT: Are there any of the Chief's decisions, from the bench, that you
      would choose to underscore?

LC: Well, I think, myself, that one that is most to his credit is the
      busing case, the city of Mecklenburg case about school busing in
      North Carolina. And he was, of course, by modern standards
      quite a liberal Republican Justice, as you know, who believed in
      affirmative action. He believed very strongly, of course, in the
      First Amendment and the Bill of Rights. He was the author of
      the *Chadha* case opinion, which was another very, very impor-
      tant case, which came back to life in this recent line-item veto
      case that one of my partners and I took part in, arguing for Sena-
      tors who opposed the line-item veto statute. [The *Chadha* deci-
      sion rejected the one-house legislative veto of executive regula-
      tions.] Another major case, where I was on the losing side, was
      the *Synar* case where I was the counsel for the Controller Gen-
      eral. I'm very critical about that opinion.

RT: You must have had a pretty good batting average with the Chief.

LC: It was pretty good. Most of the cases that I argued, or at least the
      portion I argued (as in *Buckley v. Valeo* [which focused on the
      constitutionality of certain aspects of campaign reform]), came
      out right, or at least came out on my side. My best friend on the

court was really Potter Stewart, but I didn't have better than, say, a 500 average with Potter Stewart.

RT: And what was your average with the Chief?

LC: Maybe a little bit better.

RT: The Chief was appointed by Republican presidents Eisenhower and Nixon. You were appointed White House Counsel by Democratic presidents Carter and Clinton. How did that enter, or not enter, into your relationship with him? Was it even relevant in any way?

LC: I don't think it was relevant in any way. As I say, he was not that rabid a Republican. And I was not that liberal a Democrat. But it didn't really enter into our conversations.

RT: Did you have any personal involvement with him, other than drinking wine together?

LC: Occasionally he would consult me. This was really toward the end of his life, first about his daughter, and second when Vera died and he wanted her buried in Arlington Cemetery. I was in the White House at that point.

RT: Did you arrange that? Because that was unusual, was it not, to have Vera buried there?

LC: Well, yes. The Chief would be entitled to be buried there. I don't know of any case that previously had arisen in which the Chief's spouse had died before he did. There was no trick to the solution. The President can designate burial there, and it was simply asking the President to do it.

RT: Do you know any stories or anecdotes about the Chief that are warm, touching, humorous, embarrassing, or whatever?

LC: He was not really popular among his fellow Justices, I think. But that was because he did not conduct himself as one among equals, but really as the Chief. And he put a great deal of emphasis on that. He had a Court car before any other Justice had the use of a Court car, and he chose to make the Court's conference room just outside his office into an extension of his personal office. These are things that I picked up from other Justices, law clerks, and so forth. I don't want to state any sources for any of them. He reminded me of my children who, when they put one another down, would say, "Don't be so great of yourself." And the Chief was somewhat great of himself, whereas Chief Justice Rehnquist, who was much more of a disciplinarian with the lawyers who argued cases, is liked a great deal more by all the other Justices right across the bench because he doesn't do any of those things. Court cars are now available to any Justice. But it's a minor failing. I'm sure we've had rougher Chief Justices.

RT: Do you have anything about him as a man or anything on his decisions that you wouldn't mind sharing?

LC: Bob Woodward did a lot of talking to the other Justices, and I think he has a collection of comments by the other Justices on the Chief. He wrote an article in *Esquire* if I remember correctly, after Potter Stewart died. He felt his off-the-record comments Potter had made to him could be published once Potter had died. I had a big argument with him over that because Potter's widow was very offended by all this, since all the other Justices and their wives were still there, and she saw them a lot, and here was Woodward publishing comments that Potter had made about some of the other Justices whom she continued to see.

RT: What do you think might have been public misconceptions, if any, about the Chief? Or do you think the preconceptions, whatever they were, were accurate?

LC: I think that, on the whole, the public conception was favorable. The Court has not always been trusted by most of the people. It has always been thought of as a defender of property rights rather than the rights of the poor and the underprivileged. That changed with [Chief Justice Earl] Warren. The Warren Court began upholding the rights of minorities, free speech, etc. And that was equally true of the Burger Court. The Burger Court did not really take a big shift to the right. And it was during that time that public confidence in the Court as the so-called least dangerous branch reached its height, and I think that's been maintained ever since.

RT: Why do you think he resigned?

LC: I think it was partly age. I think it was partly his enormous interest in the Constitution and the bicentenary. These pocket Constitutions are the things that he used to hand out, as you know, to everybody. And there was this sort of tacit deal that got made. The statute that created the bicentenary Commission named the Chief Justice, not by name but by office, as the chairman of the Commission. But when he resigned and Rehnquist became the Chief Justice, it was understood that Burger would continue as the Chairman of the Commission.

RT: Was that in violation of the statute, then?

INTERVIEW WITH LLOYD N. CUTLER   185

LC: One could argue that. If Rehnquist had fought for it, probably so. But it's not the kind of matter that would go to a court, I don't think. But I think it was a deal in that sense, and I think it's true of all the Justices. Some of them, like Douglas, will go on past the time when they really are able to carry the load. Others want to get out before that happens. There's a famous story about Justice Field, which goes back all the way to the Civil War and post-Civil War days. He became senile on the Court, and two of the other Justices were delegated to go speak to him, to suggest that he retire. And one of them said, "Do you remember when you and I went to see Justice so-and-so 20 or 30 years earlier and told him it was time for him to retire?" And Field's answer was, "Yes. It was the dirtiest day's work I ever did in my life." And he never got off the Court.

RT: What do you think were the Democrats' perception and the Republicans' perception of the Chief?

LC: I think the Democrats perceived him, many of them, as too conservative, and the Republicans as too liberal. But he was a true centrist on the Court.

RT: Do you have or know any stories or impressions about his good manners and diplomacy?

LC: He certainly had very good manners on the bench. And socially his manners were very good. But as you know, he abhorred television news, television in the court room, and he refused to make speeches, even before the American Bar Association, if there were television cameras present. And he was certainly not polite and charming to journalists or to the networks when they wanted to televise speeches he would make.

RT: Did you ever get an impression that he was imposing his own sense of politics on the Constitution?

LC: To the extent that all judges do. To divorce your own personal feelings from the conclusions you reach as a judge is very, very hard. There's a wonderful piece that Learned Hand wrote when Justice Cardozo died. I was the editor of the *Yale Law Journal* then, and we put out the only joint edition ever of the Yale, Harvard and Columbia law reviews, and it was all about Justice Cardozo. And in it is a piece by Learned Hand about the qualities of a judge.

RT: He told me that he personally did not approve of the death penalty, but because it was in the Constitution, he would observe it. He talked about *Roe v. Wade*, but he never talked to me about what he thought about abortion. I never asked him. I know he felt uncomfortable with that decision.

LC: He was very close to [Justice] Blackmun. As you know, they were colleagues, and Blackmun turned out to be far more liberal (or whatever you want to call it) and far more result-oriented. But I never had an abortion discussion with him. I forget how he voted on *Roe v. Wade*.

RT: He voted on the side of the majority, but whenever I talked with him about it, he was, well, defensive, apologetic. "I never meant for it to be abortion on demand," he would say. "And later on I dissented."

LC: Many people thought *Roe v. Wade* went too far. Among them was Ruth Ginsburg, who was a women's rights activist, who thought the *Roe v. Wade* rules went farther than necessary to decide the case.

RT: Any stories or impressions about his character that you haven't already discussed that you would want to mention here?

LC: No. Certainly nothing critical of his character other than vanity or self-importance, which we all suffer from.

RT: What is your understanding of his views on the Constitution? Was he satisfied with it?   He always said it was flawed, but he was a strong, strong defender of it.

LC: Of course. And he was, like Warren, very much against so-called "junk amendments" to the Constitution. I know he disliked easy amendment of the Constitution. And he was quite a literalist about the Constitution, in particular the *Chadha* case about the presentment clause, and the relationship between the President and Congress. On the other hand, under present-day conservative standards, he would have been thought of as an activist judge on all the First Amendment cases, all the affirmative action cases.

RT: If you were to rate him on a scale of liberal one and conservative ten, what would you give him?

LC: Five/six.

RT: Is there anything else that you would want to say about the Chief?

LC: I recall one aspect in particular of that trip we took [to England and Ireland] and those three oral arguments that we were in. There was no question that he was personally on one side of that case, and the quality of the argument didn't matter to him. As I recall, we split the court more or less evenly in all three arguments, and he was always on the same side. I remember suggesting to Herb Brownell at one point, that just for the fun of it, since we were going to argue it three times [at Oxford University, the Middle Temple, and the University of Dublin], why didn't we switch sides at least once? I could have argued the other side just as well. Brownell wouldn't have anything to do with that.

RT: Anything else about your friendship with the Chief?

LC: He called me up and invited me to lunch maybe three to four months before he died, and we went to the City Tavern in Georgetown. He got to talking about Vera and he literally broke into tears. He must have been—what was he—87? And this was well over a year after Vera had died, and yet he was very emotional.

RT: So that might have hastened his own death?

LC: I don't know. Well, he was clearly failing. You can see that in people. Every now and then I can see it in myself.

RT: He died a very lonely man.

LC: True. It must be true, especially after Vera died.

RT: A very lonely man. And you'd think there would be lots of people around. But I guess being Chief Justice you always maintain a kind of distance from people, don't you?

LC: That's part of the mystique of the place. How marvelous it is, but nobody calls you up. It isn't like being Assembly Leader, or Attorney General, or White House Counsel.

CHAPTER 14

INTERVIEW WITH
JUSTICE SANDRA DAY O'CONNOR

Justice Sandra Day O'Connor was nominated by President Reagan as Associate Justice of the United States Supreme Court on July 7, 1981. She was confirmed by the United States Senate on September 22, 1981 and took the oath of office on September 25, 1981. Previously, she was appointed to the Arizona Court of Appeals by Governor Bruce Babbitt and served from 1979 to 1981. She was elected judge of the Maricopa County Superior Court, Phoenix, Arizona, and served from 1975 to 1979.

Justice O'Connor was appointed State Senator in 1969 and was subsequently reelected to two two-year terms, serving in the Arizona State Senate from 1969 to 1975. She was elected Senate Majority Leader in 1972 and served as Chairman of the State, County, and Municipal Affairs Committee in 1972 and 1973. She also served on the Legislative Council, on the Probate Code Commission, and on the Arizona Advisory Council on Intergovernmental Relations.

William Webster described the Chief's reception of Justice O'Connor's nomination:

> When Justice Sandra Day O'Connor—a 1980 Anglo-American team member—was nominated to the high court, I received a call from the Chief, who was delighted. Justice O'Connor was not then the household name it is today, and he wanted to be sure that all the team members were ready to speak out on her many accomplishments and on her sterling character. A loyal friend who wanted the best for his Court and the country.

RT: The Chief would never say this, of course, but I think you were his favorite member of the Court. How did you become such good friends? Why did he have such great respect for you?

SDO: I doubt that he ranked us in terms of his favorites, but I know that he cared about me, and I know that I cared about him very much. We met one time in Arizona before I'd been thought of for the Court. He attended a conference of the Chief Justices of all the State Supreme Courts that was being held in Flagstaff, Arizona. The Chief's Administrative Assistant at the time was Mark Cannon, and Mark had a relative in Arizona who was then the mayor of Phoenix, John Driggs. Mark asked John, "Wouldn't it be a good idea to invite the Chief to Lake Powell as long as he's in Flagstaff?" Lake Powell is one of the magical places of the world. It was formed out of the Colorado River at Glen Canyon in an area that is just starkly beautiful. So John Driggs arranged to get a houseboat that slept a number of people, and through Mark Cannon, invited the Chief to Lake Powell for two or three days. And John Driggs, who is a friend of ours also, invited my husband and me to go along. We just had a fabulous time. Sometimes we would sit in inner tubes and float in the lake. And sometimes we'd fish, and sometimes we'd just sit on the houseboat as we went along. It was a great trip.

RT: Do you think that President Reagan might have queried the Chief about your nomination?

SDO: I think that could have happened. The Chief never told me that, however.

RT: What was the nature, once you were on the Court, of your continuing relationship with the Chief?

SDO: The Chief knew that I had never served in the federal court system, and that the issues coming into this Court were often new to me. And he wanted to do everything he could to help me function. I think he wanted me to have an understanding of what the Justices were expected to do, how we work; so he went out of his way to be constructive and to help and to sit down and talk about any of it. He was just terrific about that.

RT: Ken Starr said to me about the Chief, "He wanted the system to work."

SDO: He did! He cared. There are two Chief Justices in the last hundred years who really cared about the judicial system as a whole, and how it worked. One was William Howard Taft and the other was Warren Burger. Each of them really had a deep interest in making the whole system work better and in looking at the big picture. Warren Burger literally had that interest. He cared deeply about making the system in this country work as well as it could, and he did so many constructive things to help.

RT: Ken also said that it really bothered the Chief when someone within the judicial system abused it.

SDO: He was very concerned about the standards for lawyer behavior, for civility, for professionalism. He cared a lot about those things, and he cared how the courts worked to enforce them. We have a very complicated system in this country, with both the federal court system and the separate state court systems, and he cared about the interrelationship of those two. He wanted everything to function as well as it could.

RT: What was your relationship with the Chief in his final year, when he was quite ill?

SDO: As long as he came in here, of course, I would see him. His chambers were right here [next to mine], so I would see him. Occasionally we would have lunch out in the courtyard when the weather permitted. And I would see him coming by and would pop out and we'd chat or I would go by his chambers. Then when he couldn't come in, I also visited. When he was in the hospital, I visited.

RT: Is there anything that you would want to say about the Chief's views on public service?

SDO: He was a public servant from the word "go." He'd always had an interest in government and in who was running for office, and in getting qualified, decent people, and being a part of it himself. His first big political effort was on behalf of Harold Stassen; he really enjoyed that. And then, of course, he ended up here in Washington and on the Court of Appeals. He had such a sense of history and of government—more than most people. He had the big picture in mind.

RT: I asked him once what kind of a pay cut he took when he came out from Minnesota; it was staggering.

SDO: Yes. And he never complained about the fact that he wasn't earning money; he cared about serving his country and doing it well. That's clear.

RT: Is there anything you'd like to say about the Chief on his relationship with kids and young people?

SDO: He seemed to want to share with them his observations and his vision of America. He loved being Chair of the Bicentennial Commission because it gave him a platform to try to teach a new generation of young people about what it means to be an American and what the Constitution means and what our system of government means. He had traveled, and he knew comparative law and comparative systems, and he understood what we had here. He loved history.

RT: Did you ever have any surprise parties, events or ceremonies for the Chief?

SDO: I don't think I ever tried. No. That didn't strike me as a good idea. Maybe it would have been. That never occurred to me: to try a surprise.

RT: I wanted to have a birthday party for him. I got the short list of friends and worked it all out with Burnett Anderson and Mike Luttig. Then I made the mistake of telling the Chief.

SDO: I'm sure he wouldn't have it.

RT: No. But he liked the idea and initially said yes. Then he said, "But, if we invite that person, we must invite this person and this one," and finally we would have had to invite all of the city of Washington. So we had to abandon it, and I wish I hadn't, because that was the last birthday he had.

SDO: But he would have never willingly gone along with it.

RT: Oh, I know. We would have had so many noses out of joint; I know that.

SDO: That's right.

RT: I should have done it anyway.

SDO: It made sense at the time.

RT: Any stories about his sense of humor that you'd like to share?

SDO: Oh, he had a good sense of humor. I wish I were the type who could remember conversation directly, but he had just a wealth— a lifetime—of stories and experiences, and he'd share them. In the conference when we [the Justices] were together, he'd tell us humorous things.

RT: During the actual conferencing?

SDO: Yes. And when we'd have lunch, the Justices together, he'd often have stories to tell. He had a real wit and a sense of humor that showed. It was good.

RT: The Chief was a statesman, and yet he had the ability to move comfortably among ordinary people. But when the ordinary people were with him, you aspired . . .

SDO: To be better.

RT: "To be better?"

SDO: No question.

RT: So he was both above us and with us. There's a wonderful line in *Henry V*: the Captain walked among his soldiers "with cheerful semblance and sweet majesty." Doesn't "sweet majesty" fit perfectly? There was something majestic about him always.

SDO: Well, there was. He was selected out of central casting to be Chief Justice of the United States. He had the appearance, the manner, the bearing, the sense of history and his place in it to make him a perfect choice for that office.

RT: Do you have any stories about his ability to work with ordinary people?

SDO: He had to work as Chief Justice with all the people at the Court of every level to make the thing function, because he cared how the building was kept up. Maybe it was someone in the cleaning division, or someone in the police division, or someone just carrying on some ordinary task. So he tried to meet, work with, and inspire everybody at every level.

RT: You say he wouldn't consign those duties to somebody else generally?

SDO: No. No. He took enormous pride in this institution and this building, and he wanted personally to supervise the details. Every detail.

RT: Burnett Anderson said that the Chief worked hard to keep his friends. Were you able to discern that in any way? I mean, he didn't take anybody for granted, even as a friend.

SDO: He would communicate, of course. That's how you work at keeping friends: you communicate. He would call somebody up and have them come to lunch, or if within the building, come and have a cup of tea. And he would tell about things he was working on, or hope that you'd be involved in. He would maintain this flow of communication. He didn't hesitate to do that. He would call and say, "How about coming for a cup of tea, and we'll talk about . . . ."

RT: He'd initiate that then?

SDO: He would initiate. That was his way.

RT: He was reaching out.

SDO: And he would invite people that he wanted to come by from all over the city or the world, and say, "Come have lunch and talk about . . . ."

RT: I know he didn't like people arguing cases in public. I know he didn't like lawyers who advertise.

SDO: He didn't. He thought it was highly unprofessional for lawyers to talk to people from the media about pending cases. That concerned him very much and with good reason. And there were particular issues that the Court had to address where he would have strong views one way or another, and would be unhappy if it didn't turn out as he thought it should, and be pleased if it did turn out as he thought. The Chief had very high professional standards for lawyers, and he wanted every lawyer to follow them.

RT: What do you think might have been any public misconceptions about the Chief?

SDO: He didn't like to talk to the press. He tended to avoid them if he could. So the press sometimes tried to use that against him. He was perceived by some, probably, to be somewhat manipulative in his assignment of cases here. And yet, he cared a lot about how some of these issues came down. I'm sure he tried through his assignment power to have the case ultimately written in some fashion that he thought suited his own notions of how the case should be resolved.

RT: Would you say that his character was in any way complex, or even enigmatic?

SDO: Oh, of course it was. As you've already pointed out, he was very private. He didn't want to share family or personal experiences or relationships. He tended to focus on the public aspects of his life, and his experiences with judges and lawyers and political figures here and around the world, rather than on his own family, for example. And he went to his grave that way.

RT: When or where was your last meeting or conversation with the Chief?

SDO: In the hospital. At Sibley. He was very ill. We just talked about how he was feeling. I'm sure I told him what was going on at the Court and what we were doing. But he was so ill that he wasn't really focused at that time on issues. Finally, I reached over and held his hand. And we just stayed like that for maybe half an hour. He didn't want to let go. We were just there. I was holding his hand, and his eyes were closed. It was just such a sad time. I had tears flowing down my cheeks. And I had a sense of his loneliness. Vera was gone, and there wasn't anybody down there except maybe a nurse. I was profoundly sad that in his last days many of them were spent alone when here was a man who had spent his life in the public view, surrounded by people, and making decisions of every kind and description: relating to his Court, relating to the Bicentennial, relating to everything in which he was involved. Such a network of contacts and activities, and yet, here at the end, none of that. And no one there.

I think that he never knew, during their marriage, how dependent he was on Vera. He didn't talk about that. But it just seemed to me that her death before his left this enormous gap in his life that he never realized would be there.

RT: He was omnipresent in the public, and in the end nobody was there.

SDO: That's right! Which made me very sad.

RT: I used to call him and say, "Chief, I'm coming over." I didn't ask, "May I?"

SDO: I can't tell you how many times I would call when he was sick at home and say, "How about letting me come by this afternoon?" Or, "John and I would like to come," or, "We want to bring you a little hors d'oeuvre this afternoon." "Fine, fine," he'd say. Then, pretty soon, maybe an hour before we were to be there, a call would come. "Please, not today. I just can't do it today. Let's make it later in the week." There was a lot of that.

RT: If, after this interview, you think of something that you'd like to share with the people, please do let me know.

SDO: I just want people to know about what a wonderful man he was, and that the perception out there was one that was not drawn fairly about the man. I'd like to set the record straight.

CHAPTER 15

THE FINAL DAYS

I recall the Chief's final business meeting in his chambers. I set up this meeting with Frank Shakespeare, the Chief, Burnett Anderson and me to discuss adding President Bush to the Four Presidents Project. The Trust for the Bicentennial had received a grant from the Bradley Foundation, in part because of Shakespeare, who was one of the trustees of the Bradley Foundation. When I was earlier at Hillsdale College, I had known Frank as a Trustee. He had been the Ambassador to the Holy See (the Vatican) under President Bush and the Ambassador to Portugal under President Reagan. President Nixon appointed him Director of USIA, and earlier he had been a senior vice president at CBS.

For lunch that day we went to the Chief Justice's dining room. On the wall were two portraits. Frank observed that they must be portraits of famous leaders; the Chief pointed out that those were the busts of Marbury and Madison. Of course; it had to be. *Madison v. Marbury* was the landmark case that, perhaps more than any other, established the independence of the judiciary. It was the case in which Chief Justice John Marshall and the Supreme Court for the first time ruled a law of Congress unconstitutional. What more appropriate portraits than those of Madison and Marbury could grace the dining room of the Chief Justice? In the same vein, there is presently on the first floor of the Supreme Court a huge statue of John Marshall. Engraved on the wall behind him, among other of his quotations, is: "It is emphatically the province and duty of the Judicial Department to say what the law is." This independence of the judiciary is another reason the Chief would not pass through magnetometers.

As a member of the private Trust, I stayed in frequent contact with the Chief after my return to Hillsdale College. I would from time to time visit him either at the Supreme Court or at his home in Arlington, Virginia. It was sad to see the physical ravages of the man. He suffered bout after bout of respiratory infections or pneumonia and lost an alarming amount of weight. When I visited him, he would come downstairs from his bedroom in his bathrobe. We never stood on ceremony. His legs had become frightfully thin. He was severely fatigued and would sit in his study talking, frequently with his eyes closed.

Upon his death, I *had* to attend the final ceremonies. A few days before the funeral, I stood in the rain in front of the Supreme Court and watched the pallbearers carry the casket up the main front steps of the Court. No crowd was present. Only a few staffers and all members of the Supreme Court lined the steps. On the morning of the funeral, I visited his chambers in the Supreme Court. His office was crowded with judges, members of the Supreme Court, and other friends. I talked there with Justice Clarence Thomas, who narrated his affection for the Chief. He told me that when first he came to the Court, Chief Justice Burger was gracious to him, taking him by the arm and leading him throughout the Court in orientation sessions. Justice Thomas said that the Chief paid very special attention to him, making sure that he felt entirely at home in his new surrroundings.

I later attended the service at the National Presbyterian Church, then the burial at Arlington Cemetery. After the service, I watched Justice Sandra Day O'Connor unobtrusively walk sadly to the Chief's casket and place a single rose on it, then turn to hug the Chief's son, Wade.

There is no better testimony to Warren Burger's life, nor a more fitting close to this book, than Michael Luttig's eulogy:

EULOGY FOR THE HONORABLE WARREN E. BURGER
CHIEF JUSTICE OF THE UNITED STATES
BY THE HONORABLE J. MICHAEL LUTTIG
UNITED STATES COURT OF APPEALS FOR THE FOURTH CIRCUIT
JUNE 29, 1995
THE NATIONAL PRESBYTERIAN CHURCH

If ever there was a life to be celebrated, then his.

He looked like the Chief Justice of the United States. But any who think this his foremost qualification misunderstand the Office he occupied and misunderstand the man that he was.

In a society often preoccupied with politics and convinced by sound bites, not even the nature of law itself is easily understood, much less that which defines greatness in those who hold our highest judicial Office.

But history will record, as it already has begun to do, that Warren Burger was one of our great Chief Justices. It will reflect that he was exactly what the Nation wanted and needed from the one in whom it reposed this ultimate trust.

Those of us who had the privilege to serve this extraordinary man as his law clerks were well aware that we were in the service of one who rightfully held this highest of offices. Albeit from a different vantage point, we saw in him the same that his colleagues on the Court and others in private life saw.

We saw a man whose oath was virtually his faith, a man who committed his entire life to the law. We saw a man who took his duties to heart, working literally 18 to 20 hours a day, 7 days a week, year after year, in their performance.

We saw a man singularly devoted to the Constitution—his life's passion. We knew it was high allegory that this man literally handed the Constitution to hundreds of thousands of Americans during the several-year celebration of its bicentennial, just as it was fitting that he shared his birthday with that document.

We saw in this man a boundless respect—indeed, a love—for the Supreme Court. And we saw a man whose every action was calculated to bring to it respect and who tirelessly protected that institution with every ounce of his considerable energy.

We saw a man who, in an almost uncanny way, seemed guided by history, a man with enormous admiration for the Founding Fathers, who spoke of them in such a way that you believed that, somehow, some way, he really did know each and every one of them.

Perhaps most importantly, we saw a man who believed with all his heart that his high Office belonged not to him, but to the people, and that he but held it in sacred trust. We saw a man who, because of this belief, in reality was quite humbled by his great Office.

In him, we saw a man of judgment, one who had that rare gift that lies at the core of what was his life's undertaking, and for which the highest intelligence quotient is no substitute. A man who understood the difference between intellectualism for intellectualism's sake, on the one hand, and wisdom, on the other.

We saw a man of uncommon, common sense—an intensely practical man, who took pride in his practicality. One who demanded of himself opinions that could be read and understood by the people. One who never hesitated to ask, when it made no sense at all, "Can this really be the law?"

We saw a man with a fierce sense of justice, a man who, one summer night in London, would not be restrained from entering and breaking up a street brawl when he saw five young thugs beating a lone other with fists and sticks. The Chief Justice. "It just wasn't right," he said.

In him, we saw a man who eschewed labels and denied categorization. There was no mistaking that Warren Burger was independent, that he was his own man, in everything he did.

There was never a doubt as to where the Chief Justice stood on an issue, from the need to turn off the lights during the energy crisis (of which we were reminded by hand-scrawled orders taped to the switchplates) to the loftiest constitutional issue.

And, in keeping, we saw a man who simply declined to mold his own image through the avenues of media.

We, too, saw a "visionary." A traditional, conventional man, but a man who, from his professional days in St. Paul, was never comfortable doing it "that way" just because "it had always been done that way." A man who, although inspired by history, was never fearful of challenging even the tried and tested, which he frequently did with that familiar twinkle in his eye. He was challenged, and he challenged others, to do better, in the administration of the courts, in prison reform, in effective judicial decision-making. There was nothing as to which he refused to take a "fresh look."

He was a man who saw it as his solemn obligation to tout the virtues of the American system of law, here and abroad which, because he was convinced of those virtues, was easy to do. If told that he never turned down a request to discuss his favorite subjects—American law and the Constitution—I would believe. There was never a discussion, never a speech, when our reforms, our progress, our achievements were not hailed by him and held up as exemplary.

And throughout our years with him, we saw a man of deep conviction and the certain strength that almost always attends such conviction. A man who had the courage and the character to stand up for what he believed was right. A man who, as all here would attest, never failed to speak his mind for fear of criticism.

And in this unmistakable strength, this strength of character, we saw, and we sensed, a steadiness and a balance that reassured us, as it did the Country, that our faith in the institutions of government, and particularly the judiciary, was fully justified. And all the while we understood that under his leadership, the course of law, and thereby the course of history, was undergoing a slow, but assuredly fundamental change.

We also had the opportunity to see "the Chief" just as a person, without the mantle of office. (Chief Justices, we forget, are people, too.) We saw what those who knew him only as a public figure never saw. And in many ways, this was the most special aspect of our service.

We saw a man who was easily understood—but only if one cared to understand.

We saw not at all a private man in the sense that was thought, but rather a man who always loved to be with and around people—visitors in the halls of the Court, acquaintances from the Washington establishment, and old friends—a man who simply treasured the very, very few hours a week he did allow himself and his family.

We saw a man who was supremely conscious of the magnitude of the responsibilities he had assumed and the little time that there was to fulfill them in the way he had decided they must be fulfilled, but a man who ultimately was very much at ease with himself and his Office.

We saw a man who, though comfortable with formality, much preferred informality. A man whose austere lifestyle never fell prey to official Washington. A man who, though he spent a lifetime in this Capital City, in important respects never lost the quaintness of his earliest Minnesotan home.

We saw, evident in everything he did, those wonderful, enduring midwestern values. A man with a profound sense of right and wrong, he was. In a time when it seemed that all had become relative, it simply was never so for him.

We saw a man whose respite was in tending to what seemed like the tiniest details of internal court management—details he took the time to address so that the public could better understand the Supreme Court and its role in our democracy.

We saw the man who, for hours, could recount story after story from history in such vivid detail that you would swear you were there.

We saw this man of commanding presence, who, for reasons we are only now beginning to understand, seemed never to hold a child or to speak of an old friend without tears coming to his eyes.

We also saw, up close, the quiet but true love he had for Vera, who was his strength, and we saw the equally intense fatherly love that he had for Wade and for Margaret.

We saw the fiery patriotism of a man who loved his Country as much as anyone could.

We saw the wide connoisseur, the chef (whose bean soup and orange marmalade were nationally known—at least among his law clerks), the artist, the sculptor, the naturist (who delighted that the same birds that nested in his holly tree on Rochester Street found their way to his new home on Wakefield), the antique buff, the humorist, and the political observer.

We saw much more that, because of his Office, was regrettably hard for others to see.

And as we watched, we caught his contagious enthusiasm for life.

In a word, if only briefly, we who had the privilege of serving the Chief Justice were able to see the law—and life—through the eyes of an elegant, graceful patriot. And what an inspirational perspective it was!

He has now passed this life. But is there any doubt that he lives on through the institutions he shaped and so very much cherished, and through the countless lives he touched? A richer legacy than his none of us could hope for.

If ever there was a life to be celebrated, then his.

I remember well my last time with the Chief. I called him and said I was coming to Washington "on business" and wanted to stop by and see him. That was mostly a fib: I arranged the business trip really to see him. He did not object to my intrusion; he never did. The lone maid answered the doorbell; Mrs. Burger was now gone. The Chief came downstairs in robe and pajamas, fatigued, pale and shockingly thin. He had recently been hospitalized for pneumonia. We talked for a while, saying nothing. Soon his eyes closed, and he leaned his head back against the high wingback chair. For a while he was able to look at me when speaking, but now he spoke haltingly with his eyes closed. Then he stopped and was asleep. I got up quietly, got my coat, and let myself out the door.

I never saw him again. I never said good-bye.